# BT-13A
# BASIC TRAINER

## STUDENTS' MANUAL

Prepared by the

ARMY AIR FORCES TRAINING COMMAND

Visual Training Unit, in collaboration with the

CENTRAL INSTRUCTORS SCHOOL

Randolph Field, Texas and

HEADQUARTERS, AAF, OFFICE OF FLYING SAFETY

Safety Education Division

TO BE USED IN CONJUNCTION WITH THE CURRENT AAF TRAINING COMMAND MEMORANDUM

COVERING BASIC FLYING TRAINING

*Foreword*

★ You have successfully completed the first part of the training that will ultimately qualify you as a competent airplane commander—ready for combat assignment. There are several considerations important to your progress in Basic Training.

★ **Keep your eyes on the ultimate objective—combat competence.** Eventually you will be called upon to put into practice the knowledge, skill and experience you are now accumulating hour by hour, day by day. If, throughout your course in Basic Training, you will strive to see the combat applications of the training you are receiving, you will be repaid many times.

★ **Learn with all your might.** Your program of training is based on the accumulated experience of millions of hours of military flying. But skill and judgment are not handed out on a silver platter. You have to work for them and work **hard.** The necessarily rapid pace of all phases of flying training calls for a maximum contribution of time and effort on your part.

★ It calls also for an attitude of mind which stores away and remembers each day's progress. For only in that way can you acquire the complete mastery of flying that is essential to your success.

★ **Use this Manual.** It was prepared to speed your progress and to provide a handy source of information which, if properly used on the ground, will greatly multiply the benefits of hours spent in the air.

★ Always keep in mind that the training you are receiving is the same or even better than the training that produced the pilots who are now carrying the battle to the enemy. If you apply yourself conscientiously and intelligently day by day, there can be no doubt of the final result.

Lieutenant General, U.S.A.
Commanding

3

# A Tip on Pilots

## FROM MARK TWAIN

"A pilot must have a memory developed to absolute perfection," Mark Twain once wrote. "But there are two higher qualities which he also must have. He must have good and quick judgment and decision, and a cool, calm courage that no peril can shake."

Mark Twain was writing not of airplane pilots but of men who steered Mississippi River stern wheelers which often attained the terrifying speed of 14 MILES PER HOUR.

*Now!*

In Primary Training you were introduced to airplanes and learned certain fundamentals of flying. Now you are taking off on the most important leg of your flying training—Basic Training. Do a bang-up job and you'll be well on your way toward a perfect landing in a P-38 or a B-24 that is scheduled for combat duty.

Basic Training is your opportunity to learn precision, maximum performance flying. Pilots who treat flying as a hobby can get by without knowing the fine points, but military pilots must develop a master touch and be able to get the utmost in performance out of their airplanes. You are training for a championship bout in which there are no holds barred, and the skill you acquire depends largely upon how diligently you are willing to work for it. You want your wings, but a hundred times more important is the skill that those wings symbolize. Out of every class there is at least one student who "just made it" and there is another who is "tops" because he has squeezed every hour for all it was worth to become a better pilot. Which would you rather be, and which would you rather have on your wing in a formation of fighters or as your copilot in a B-17?

5

Basic Training is brief, only ten weeks. You will probably find yourself busier than you have ever been in your life. That sort of thing is inevitable in time of war. The enemy won't wait around while Uncle Sam conducts a leisurely pilot training program. Your training is rapid but it is the finest pilot training in the world. Everyone at your field, from the Commanding Officer down to the boys who wash the airplanes, is doing everything in his power to help you become a better pilot. If the program sometimes seems impersonal or rigid, be generous enough to realize that everyone is carrying a heavy load of responsibilities.

## PURPOSE OF BASIC MANEUVERS

Every maneuver and operation in Basic Training has a fighting purpose. You won't realize the full significance of this statement until you start making practice bombing runs or shooting at a tow target in a P-38. A slight slip or skid will raise cain with a gunnery score. And a bombardier is just as concerned with his pilot's touch on the controls as he is with the accuracy of his bombsight. Each maneuver you are taught is a step toward more advanced air work.

The Approach To A Stall, for example, is a step toward the Maximum Performance Climbing Turn which is preliminary to Chandelles, etc. You have to know stalls before you can make good landings or properly fly a Hurdle Stage. The successful graduate from Basic School knows how to get the most out of an airplane and can apply what he has learned to other types of aircraft. Don't slight anything with the idea that it isn't important. **In combat flying everything is important.**

# YOUR INSTRUCTOR

Your instructor is a well-qualified military pilot. He knows the Basic Trainer and he knows the maneuvers. His main job is to graduate expert pilots to the next stage of training. The one thing he lacks is time. The program of pilot training has expanded so rapidly that it has been impossible to supply as many instructors as is desirable. As a result some instructors must train more students than they would have in peacetime. Carrying a heavy schedule, it is only natural for an instructor to expect every student to give his best efforts. Learn all you can on the ground during spare time, and your time in the air will be that much more productive.

## BE READY TO FLY

Nothing will disturb your instructor more than to be all set to take you up and not be able to find you, to find that you are short some of your equipment, or that you have not prepared for the flight. This is not grade school. Student pilots are selected for initiative, resourcefulness, and intelligence. Officers in the Air Forces are expected to keep alert, to think ahead, and to be ready for the unexpected. If you are eager, interested, and enthusiastic, you'll find that your instructor will reflect your enthusiasm and try that much harder to help you all he can. Flying is fun! The more you put into it and the greater your skill, the more fun you get out of it.

## ASK QUESTIONS

The only way to find out things is to ask questions. If some problem has you buffaloed, get it off your chest. An unanswered question in the back of your mind can seriously interfere with your progress. Don't be afraid of appearing ignorant. Pilots with 10,000 hours of experience are still asking questions and still learning. No one knows everything about flying and never will. By asking questions on the ground you can save time in the air.

READ IT!

APPLY IT!

REVIEW IT!

## HOW TO USE THIS MANUAL

This manual was prepared to help you become a better pilot. What you read here will round out what your instructor tells and shows you. To get the most out of an hour's flying, first learn all you can about the operation on the ground. Study it, listen carefully to what your instructor has to say; see it demonstrated in the air, and then try it yourself. Then, when you are back on the ground, review what the manual said about the problem and try to figure out what you will do next time to correct any errors you may have made.

Read from day to day about those operations and maneuvers that are coming up next. Keep your manual handy. If some change in the program gives you a spare hour, study this book! Learn more about radio, lazy eights, night navigation, climbing turns, or whatever you will be practicing next.

### IF IT'S IN THE MANUAL, YOU'RE EXPECTED TO KNOW IT!

## EQUIPMENT

Get a well-fitting parachute. Serious injuries can result from poorly fitting chutes (see parachute section). Be sure your goggles don't distort your vision and that your helmet or earphones fit properly. You can't learn if you can't hear. If you have trouble understanding your instructor in the air, tell him immediately. He will help you figure out the difficulty.

To do his best, a pilot must have well-fitting, serviceable equipment. Check yours carefully and change it if necessary.

## SIGNALS

Since you will fly from the front cockpit, hand signals are not practical and the interphone will be used almost exclusively. Remember the interphone is for listening... not for idle conversation. If the airplane is equipped with a mirror, two signals may be useful:

1. The instructor will shake the stick to get your attention and point to his **head** meaning that he has it.

2. The instructor will shake the stick pointing at you and meaning you've got it. You shake the stick acknowledging that you have it.

*Who's Got It?*

Students should stay on the controls always and keep flying the airplane every minute unless specifically told otherwise. Confusion over **who** is doing the flying is dangerous and must be avoided. Fly as if you were flying solo unless you **know** the instructor wants the controls.

## USE OF SPARE TIME

Nothing will get you off to a good start as much as proper use of spare time during the first week or so of your Basic Training. You have a new airplane and new traffic patterns to learn about and a new area in which to do your flying.

Sit in the airplane every chance you get. "Dry run" through various procedures. With the checklist in your hand and a little imagination, you can go through many of the pre-solo requirements by simply pointing at the different controls in the sequence you would use them. This will pay real dividends in the air. You will soon know the Basic Trainer as well as you know the palm of your right hand.

Memorize the traffic patterns quickly. Erase other patterns from your mind and learn these new ones. Orient the pattern with the field itself so that you will immediately catch on to your instructor's explanations. If he finds you are "doing your darndest," he will be more patient and try that much harder to speed your progress.

On the first or second day you will get an orientation ride. Your instructor will point out the auxiliary fields, limits of the area, and principal landmarks. Study the map of the area in advance so you know what to look for. Then you won't be embarrassed by getting lost in your own back yard.

There is excellent source material to read in your spare time. You can't learn to fly out of a book, but there is a lot of reading matter that will help you.

TECHNICAL ORDER NO 01-50BC-1

## BT-13A and SNV-1
### AIRPLANES
•
*PILOT'S*

*FLIGHT OPERATING INSTRUCTIONS*

NOTICE: This document contains information affecting the National Defense of the United States within the meaning of the Espionage Act, 50 U. S. C., 31 and 32, as amended. Its transmission or the revelation of its contents in any manner to an unauthorized person is prohibited by law.

PUBLISHED BY AUTHORITY OF THE COMMANDING GENERAL,
ARMY AIR FORCES, BY THE HEADQUARTERS,
AIR SERVICE COMMAND, PATTERSON FIELD, FAIRFIELD, OHIO

The A L Garber Co., Ashland, O  3-43, 17,000

*MARCH 15, 1943*

1. There is a Technical Order for every airplane entitled **Pilot's Flight Operating Instructions.** It is prepared to help the pilot do a better job of flying the airplane. These technical orders are always numbered No. 01-, etc. The one for the BT-13A, for example, is No. 01-50BC-1. You should find it in the data case in your airplane. This is one of the greatest helps in checking out in a strange airplane whether it is a PT-17 or a B-29.

2. Pilots' Information File. You'll find copies of PIF in the ready room. It is a pilot's bible — a compilation of the best ideas of army and civilian fliers. Don't try to read it through from front to back. Turn to the sections on your immediate problems: Take-offs, Air Traffic Rules, Radio, Stalls, Spins, etc.

3. The manual for your own field will contain rules you will be expected to know. Study it and ask about anything you don't understand.

4. Your flying instructor and ground school instructors can suggest other helpful sources of information.

# HOLD ON TIGHT

The first few days at Basic School may put you in a whirl. A whole lot is thrown at students in a short time. Learn as much as you can as fast as you can. If the going gets heavy, remember that hundreds of guys just like yourself have successfully completed this same stage of training. Give your best and your instructor will do his best to see you through.

### HERE ARE TIPS THAT WILL STEP-UP YOUR PROGRESS:

1. BE EAGER! Don't let anybody or anything keep you from learning all you can.

2. BE FIT! Don't come to the flight line worn out because it's a "morning after"!

3. BE READY! Read this manual and find out those things that will help you during tomorrow's flight.

4. VISUALIZE! A clear mental picture of a maneuver will help you to execute it. Don't be a robot! Don't copy your instructor's application of controls. Visualize the maneuver and use controls to put the airplane through that maneuver.

5. ANALYZE! Be critical of your own flying. Learn to analyze your errors and correct them.

6. BREAK EACH OPERATION UP INTO STEPS. Do things in an orderly sequence. That is the easiest way to learn and remember.

7. MASTER THE SMALL THINGS. Advanced air work is a combination of less complicated operations and maneuvers.

8. DISCUSS YOUR PROBLEMS with your fellow students and your instructor. Two heads are better than one.

9. KEEP NOTES; review your notebook frequently. A good pilot knows a lot besides stick and rudder.

10. DON'T GET DISCOURAGED. Keep banging away and you'll knock your worries for a loop.

# Features
## OF THE BASIC TRAINER

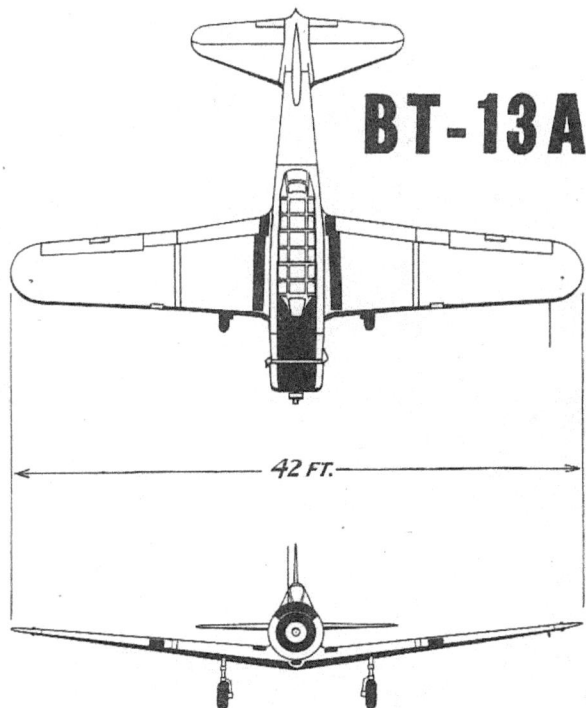

**BT-13A**

42 FT.

28 FT. 10 IN.

Your new airplane is a **good** airplane. It's easy to fly but not easy to fly expertly and that is the main object of Basic Training, to teach you precision flying. If you have any questions or doubts about the Basic Trainer, state them frankly to your instructor.

It is important to **know your airplane!** Here is an example of the kind of information you should learn about any airplane you are learning to fly. Facts given here are for the BT-13A. Get the facts for the type of airplane used in your school.

**ENGINE:** Pratt & Whitney, 9-cylinder, radial, air-cooled, direct drive type, developing 450 hp. at sea level.

**PROPELLER:** Hamilton Standard 2-blade, hydrocontrollable 2-position type, 9 ft. in diameter. Low-pitch 12.5°. High pitch 18°.

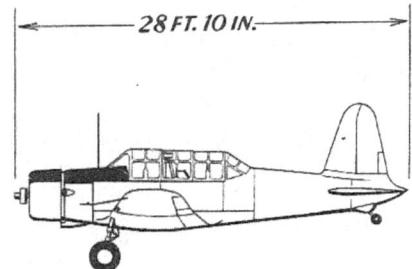

11

**WINGS:** Cantilever type, symmetrical airfoil internally braced, covered with semi-stressed skin; with 60-gallon gas tanks built into each wing. Pronounced dihedral (wings at an angle up 7° from a horizontal plane) gives extra stability in flight.

**AILERONS:** Move up 25° or 4½"; move down 11½° or 2". Equipped with Servo tabs not adjustable from the cockpit.

**FLAPS:** Slotted type forming 25 percent of the wing chord. Move down 60° maximum or 16½".

**RUDDER:** Moves 35° each side of neutral. Equipped with trim tab adjustable from the cockpit.

**VERTICAL STABILIZER:** Symmetrical airfoil fixed at 0°.

**ELEVATORS:** Move up 30° or approximately 9½". Move down 25° or 8¼". Equipped with trim tabs adjustable from control in the cockpit.

**HORIZONTAL STABILIZER:** Symmetrical airfoil set at an angle 1½° positive, i.e., nose up.

**TAILWHEEL:** Steerable. Connected with rudder throughout arc through which rudder moves. Then swivels free but will re-engage when brought back within the rudder arc.

**LANDING GEAR:** Strong, wide, fixed gear equipped with hydraulic wheel brakes.

# VISUAL INSPECTION

Always make it a practice to walk entirely around the airplane with your eyes taking in every detail before you get in the cockpit. You may do this dozens of times without finding anything wrong. But maintenance men and your fellow pilots are only human and can make mistakes. You only have to take off once with a loose gas tank cap, the baggage compartment unlocked, or a piece of cowling ready to fly off, to realize the value of visually inspecting the outside of the airplane. The day you neglect the visual inspection will probably be the same day that your instructor intentionally leaves a gas tank cap unfastened. Then he'll say, **"Are you sure you are all ready to go flying, mister?"** This is a good time to get out of the airplane and find out what you have overlooked. It is probably your pitot tube cover or something equally obvious. With this cover on, you might as well throw your airspeed indicator away.

Don't forget to check the rear cockpit when flying solo. A loose safety belt, shoulder harness, headset, or microphone can jam the controls or cause damage. These are only common sense precautions that are second nature to seasoned pilots.

I DUG A DITCH ONCE!

# Cockpit of the BT-13

Before you solo you will be required to pass a Blindfold Cockpit Check, so get acquainted with the cockpit of your new airplane. Find out where everything is, what it's for, and how to use it. The way to learn the cockpit is to sit in the airplane, study the controls and instruments, read up on them, and ask questions.

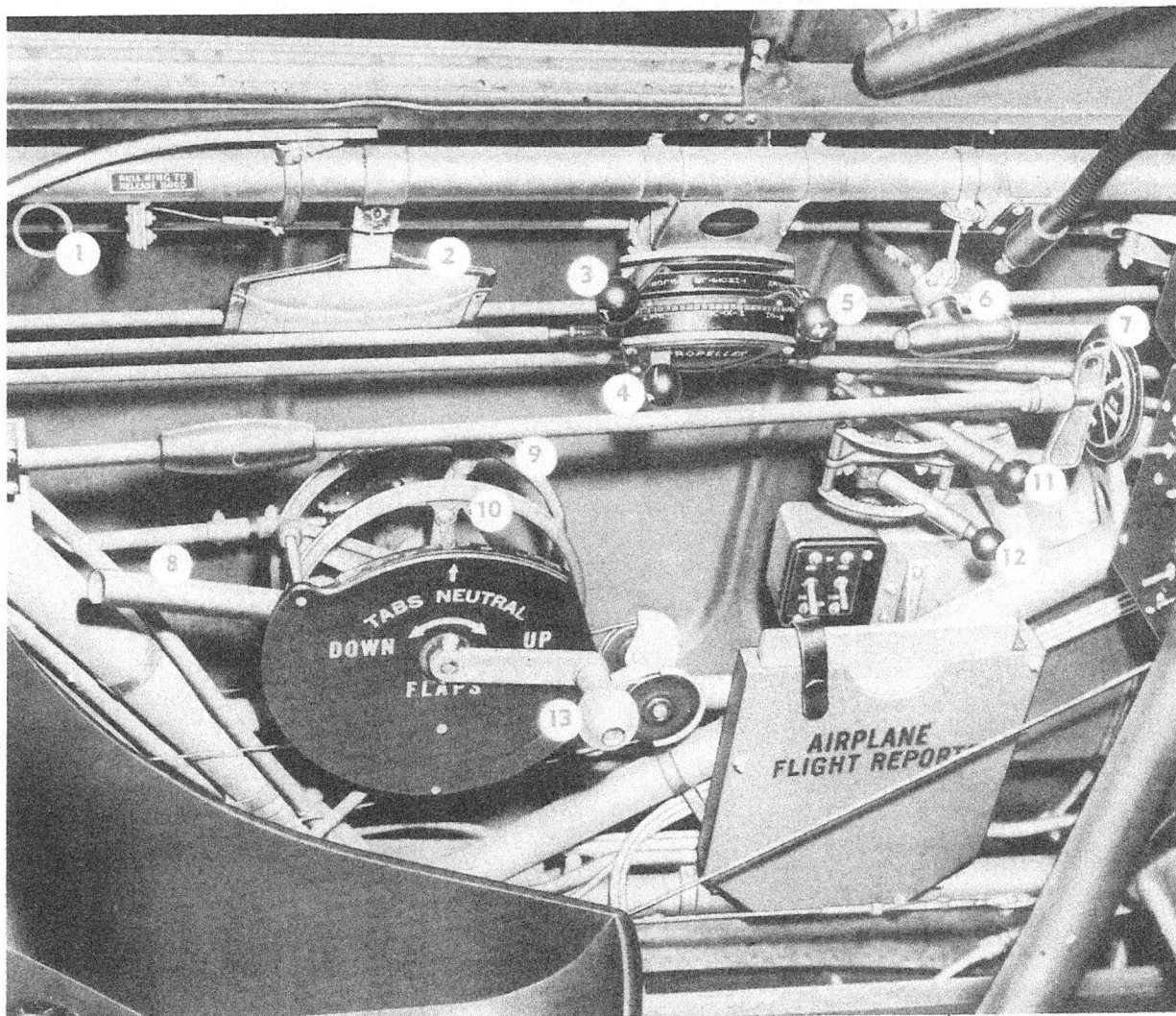

## LEFT SIDE OF FRONT COCKPIT

1. Blind Flying Hood Release.
2. Pilots' Checklist.
3. Throttle.
4. Propeller Control.
5. Mixture Control.
6. Cockpit Spotlight.
7. Fuel Tank Selector Valve Control.
8. Wobble Pump Handle.
9. Rudder Trim Tab Control.
10. Elevator Trim Tab Control.
11. Carburetor Heat Control.
12. Oil Cooler Shutter Control.
13. Flap Handle.

FRONT COCKPIT
INSTRUMENT PANEL
AND CONTROLS

| | | |
|---|---|---|
| 1. Fluorescent Lamp. | 12. Suction Gage. | 23. Cockpit Hot and Cold Air Control. |
| 2. Free Air Temperature Gage. | 13. Clock. | 24. Vacuum Restrictor Valve. |
| 3. Directional Gyro. | 14. Oil Dilution Control. | 25. Parking Brake Handle. |
| 4. Fuel Pressure Warning Light. | 15. Carburetor Mixture Temp. Gage. | 26. Radio Fuse Box. |
| 5. Artificial Horizon. | 16. Cylinder Head Temperature Gage. | 27. L-H Rudder Pedal Adjustment Lever. |
| 6. Compass. | 17. Engine Gage Unit. | 28. L-H Rudder Pedal. |
| 7. Primer. | 18. Tachometer. | 29. Control Stick Assembly. |
| 8. Altimeter. | 19. Ignition Switch. | 30. Control Lock (Stowed). |
| 9. Airspeed Indicator. | 20. Static Pressure Valve. | 31. Cockpit Hot and Cold Air Diffuser. |
| 10. Turn and Bank Indicator. | 21. Spare Lamps. | 32. R-H Rudder Pedal. |
| 11. Rate of Climb Indicator. | 22. Electrical Control Panel. | 33. R-H Rudder Pedal Adjustment Lever. |

## RIGHT SIDE OF FRONT COCKPIT

1. Transmitter Control Unit (Voice, CW, or Tone).
2. Receiver Control Unit (Auto, Off, or Manual).
3. Receiver Tuning Control.
4. Filter Unit (Voice, Range, or Both).
5. Radio Interphone Switch.
6. Radio Transmitter.
7. Cockpit Spotlight.
8. Microphone.
9. Radio Receiver.
10. High-Low Coil Switch.
11. Map Case.
12. Relief Tube.
13. Seat Height Adjustment Lever.

# COCKPIT
## *Checklist*

A checklist of this type is secured in the cockpit of each Basic Trainer. Go over the checklist word by word again and again. In a few days you'll know it by heart. When you learn the checklist so well that you do the right thing almost automatically, your progress will be much more rapid.

Don't ever get so "sharp" you are ashamed to refer to the checklist. Refresh your memory often and get in the habit of using the checklist. It is indispensable to the safe operation of larger aircraft. The pilot who is so "hot" he never needs the checklist is too "hot" for tactical equipment.

## PILOT'S CHECKLIST

**BT-13 Airplanes and BT-13A Airplanes**
**Pratt & Whitney R-985-AN-1 and 3**
**Use CAPITALIZED words for routine checking**

### ★ BEFORE ENTERING COCKPIT

1. Check PITOT TUBE for COVER, OLEO STRUTS, HYDRAULIC LINES, and TIRES.
2. Check for LOOSE COWLINGS, PANELS, etc.
3. Check REAR COCKPIT if solo. Fasten SAFETY BELT and SHOULDER HARNESS. Check for LOOSE ITEMS (headset, microphone, instrument hood, etc.) Cage GYRO INSTRUMENTS if ACROBATICS are planned.

### ★ BEFORE STARTING ENGINE

1. Check FORM 1A. Fill out FORM 1.
2. Set PARKING BRAKE. Unlock CONTROLS and secure CONTROL LOCK in FLOOR CLIP.
3. Carburetor Heat COLD.
4. Oil Cooler Shutter OPEN.
5. Battery disconnect and Generator switch ON (in airplanes so equipped).
6. Ignition switch OFF.
7. Mixture control FULL RICH.
8. Propeller Control BACK (low rpm).
9. Throttle set ¾ in. OPEN.
10. Check FUEL SUPPLY. Selector Valve on RESERVE.

### ★ STARTING ENGINE

1. WOBBLE PUMP Fuel Pressure to 3 or 4 lbs.
2. PRIME engine (7 to 9 strokes maximum; little or none for hot engine).
3. Ignition switch ON.
4. Maintain FUEL PRESSURE with WOBBLE PUMP until engine starts. CAUTION: DO NOT PUMP THROTTLE.

## DURING WARM-UP

1. After OIL GAGE indicates PRESSURE, run engine at 600 to 800 rpm. CAUTION: IF OIL PRESSURE is not indicated within 30 seconds—STOP ENGINE.
2. Move Propeller Control FORWARD (high rpm) after 60 lbs. pressure is indicated and warm up at 1,000 rpm.
3. OIL PRESSURE 75 to 90 lbs.; maximum, 100 lbs.; minimum, 60 lbs.; idling, 15 lbs.
4. OIL TEMPERATURE 50° to 70° C.; maximum 95° C.
5. FUEL PRESSURE 3 to 4 lbs.
6. Check ENGINE and MAGNETOS at 1,500 rpm. Maximum drop on either magneto, 100 rpm.
7. Check GENERATOR and electric SWITCHES, VOLTMETER and AMMETER.
8. RADIO tuned to tower; Volume UP.

## BEFORE TAKE-OFF

1. Check CONTROLS for free movement.
2. Engine controls:
   Mixture FULL RICH.
   Oil Cooler Shutter OPEN.
   CARBURETOR HEAT as required.
   Propeller Control FORWARD (high rpm).
   Check GASOLINE quantity. FUEL SELECTOR VALVE set for RIGHT TANK on first flight after REFUEL. Subsequent take-offs on tank with MOST GAS, either Left or Reserve.
3. Engine RUN UP full rpm. Unit gage readings:
   OIL PRESSURE, 75 to 90 lbs.; Minimum OIL TEMPERATURE, 30° C.; FUEL PRESSURE, 3 to 4 lbs.
4. POWER LIMIT 2,300 rpm for take-off.
5. Set RUDDER and ELEVATOR TABS at 0°.
6. Flaps DOWN 10 turns, 20°.

## DURING FLIGHT

1. CLIMB 20° FLAPS, high rpm. Normal climb 90 mph.
2. OIL COOLER SHUTTER and CARBURETOR HEAT adjusted for proper temperature.
3. Keep FUEL TANKS EQUALIZED within 10 gallons; alternate between LEFT and RESERVE.
4. Maximum DIVING SPEED 230 mph and 2,400 rpm.
5. ALLOWABLE ENGINE OPERATION
   Climb and High Speed—Maximum rpm, 2,300.
   Mixture Control—FULL RICH.
   Climb—Desired rpm, 2,100.
   Cruising—Low rpm; desired rpm, 1,900; maximum rpm, 2,000; mixture control, Full Rich to Smooth Operation.

## BEFORE LANDING

1. RADIO tuned to tower; volume UP.
2. FUEL SELECTOR VALVE on tank with MOST FUEL, either Left or Reserve.
3. Mixture FULL RICH.
4. Propeller Control FORWARD (high rpm).
5. Check CARBURETOR HEAT.
6. Flaps as needed. (Do not lower if airspeed is over 120 mph).

## AFTER LANDING

NOTE: This engine is equipped with an "Idle Cut-off."
1. FLAPS UP when taxiing.
2. Use OIL DILUTION as required.
3. IDLE Engine at 800 to 1,000 rpm. Move Propeller Control BACK (low rpm).
4. Place MIXTURE CONTROL in "IDLE CUT-OFF."
5. Turn all SWITCHES OFF when PROPELLER STOPS.
6. Set PARKING BRAKE. Lock CONTROLS.
7. Do not hang RADIO HEADSET near Instrument Panel.

# PRECAUTIONS

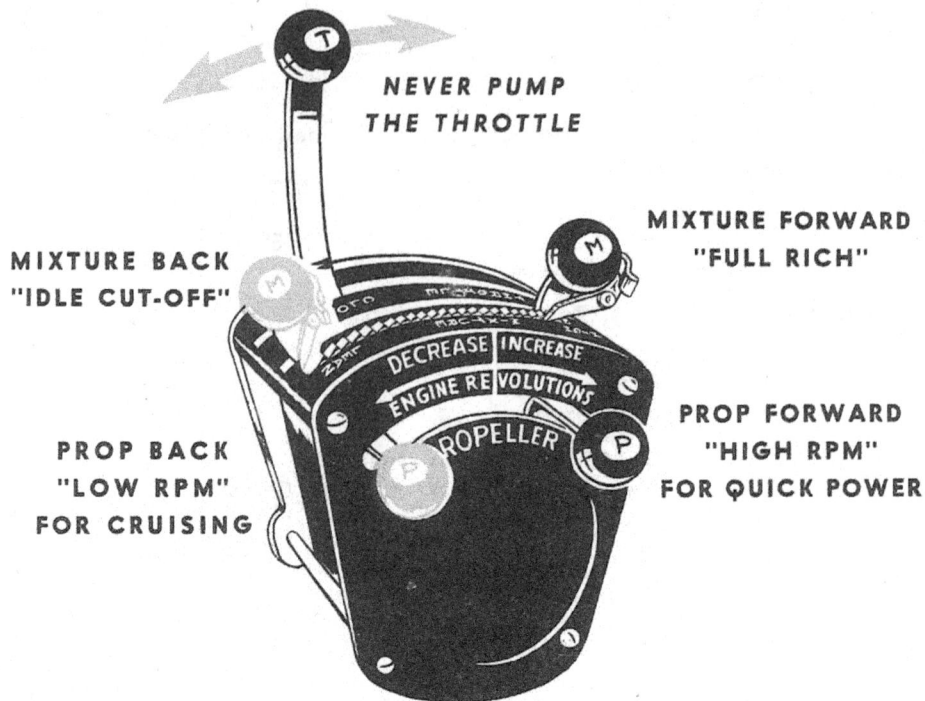

NEVER PUMP
THE THROTTLE

MIXTURE BACK
"IDLE CUT-OFF"

MIXTURE FORWARD
"FULL RICH"

DECREASE   INCREASE
ENGINE REVOLUTIONS

PROPELLER

PROP BACK
"LOW RPM"
FOR CRUISING

PROP FORWARD
"HIGH RPM"
FOR QUICK POWER

## KNOW THE THROTTLE QUADRANT THOROUGHLY

Following are general precautions to remember when operating the BT-13A:

### Throttle

Never pump or prime with the throttle. This may cause gas to leak out of the carburetor into the cowl and catch fire.

### Mixture Control

All the way forward. Mixture Control partially back leans the mixture, which may cause detonation, loss of power, and overheating. When the Mixture Control is all the way back, the engine will **stop** immediately because it is equipped with an Idle Cut-Off which stops the flow of fuel.

### Propeller Control

Forward for High rpm and quick power after the engine is warmed up. All three controls in the throttle quadrant should be in the full forward position for maximum, quick power. Just before shutting off engine, move propeller control to Low rpm long enough for propeller to change to Low rpm position.

"FEEL THE CLICK"

### Fuel Tank Selector

Learn to FEEL the click to be sure pointer is in the right position for unrestricted gas flow. Be sure the **pointer** and not the **handle** is on the desired tank.

### Fuel Pressure Warning Lamp

Always check the glow during warm-up to be sure the globe is not burned out.

"BE SURE
IT'S LOCKED"

LOCKED

UNLOCKED

### Primer

Always lock the primer immediately after priming; otherwise fuel may leak and create a fire hazard or will greatly increase fuel consumption, since extra fuel will be forced into the top five cylinders through the primer lines.

### Fire

If fire should pour out of the exhaust, keep engaged and smoothly open the throttle. When the engine starts, the fire will blow out.

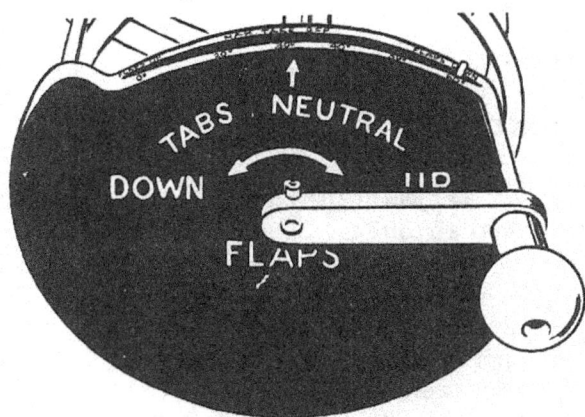

TABS   NEUTRAL

DOWN   UP

FLAPS

### Flap Control

One turn of the crank equals approximately 2° of flaps. Flaps should never be down when airspeed exceeds 120 mph.

### Carburetor Heat Control

Far more damage can result from improper use than from none at all. Don't use it until you learn how.

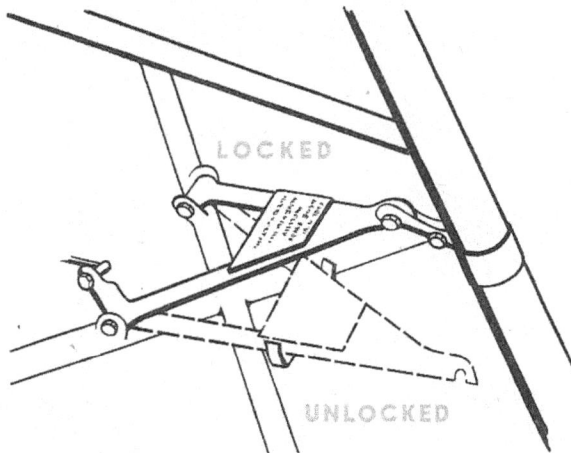

### Control Lock

Must be firmly clipped down when controls are unlocked or it can snap up during flight and jam the controls.

TO SET BRAKES

1. **DEPRESS PEDALS AND HOLD**
2. **PULL BRAKE HANDLE**
3. **RELEASE PEDALS**
4. **RELEASE HANDLE**

TO RELEASE BRAKES

1. **DEPRESS PEDALS**

### Parking Brakes

Must be set before the airplane is started and when it is parked, but released before taxiing.

### Headset

Don't hang the headset near the instrument panel. Instruments will become magnetized and won't function properly.

### CAUTION

Avoid prolonged running at or near full throttle on the ground because cooling is insufficient. Engine should not be flown if it turns up less than 1,850 rpm at full throttle on the ground.

# QUESTIONS AND ANSWERS

**1. Q. What are the forces acting on an airplane in flight?**

A. Lift, thrust, drag, and weight or gravity.

**2. What is roll? ... pitch? ... yaw?**

A. When the wingtips dip up and down, the airplane is rolling; when the nose dips up and down, the airplane is pitching; when the nose swings right or left, the airplane is yawing to the right or left.

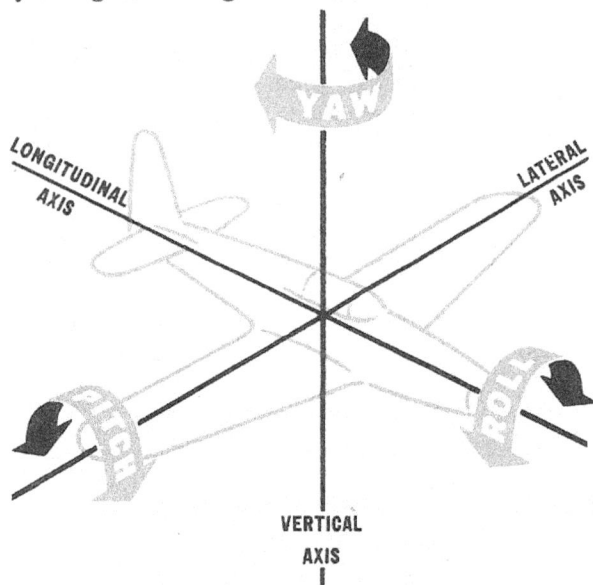

LONGITUDINAL AXIS

LATERAL AXIS

VERTICAL AXIS

**3. Q. What is a slip? ... a skid?**

A. This is best explained by example. If a turn is made too fast in an automobile on a flat road, the car tends to skid toward the outside of the turn. If the road were banked the correct amount (the degree depending on the speed of the car and the sharpness of the turn), the car would shoot smoothly around the curve. But if the road is steeply banked and the car is proceeding slowly the car tends to slip down toward the inside of the turn. These same principles apply to flying. An airplane slips or skids in turns if control pressures are not properly coordinated to establish and hold the correct bank for the rate of turn. Good coordination eliminates slips and skids.

**4. Q. How is the BT-13A rigged to correct for torque in cruising flight?**

A. Aileron tabs are adjusted manually on the ground to compensate for the rolling effect of torque at cruising speed and rpm. This is different from torque corrections in which the left wing is washed in and the leading edge of the vertical stabilizer is offset to the left. In the BT-13A the wings are identical and the vertical stabilizer is not offset. Adjustments of rudder tab are made from the cockpit to trim the airplane for various conditions of flight (similar to use of elevator trim tab control).

## SYMMETRICAL

## CONVENTIONAL

**5. Q. Does the BT-13A have a conventional airfoil?**

A. No. The airfoil section is symmetrical, i.e., the wing has the same curve and shape (camber) on the under surface as on the upper surface. This results in an efficient wing at cruising speeds.

**6. Q. Is the BT-13A airfoil as efficient at low speed with flaps up as with flaps down?**

A. No. The airfoil is more efficient with the correct amount of flaps down for the particular type of performance desired, because flaps change the airfoil, increase the lift, and decrease the stalling speed. Flaps provide excellent flight characteristics at low airspeeds in the BT-13A.

**7. Q. What two forces are set up by application of ailerons only?**

A. Roll and yaw opposite to the roll.

8. Q. In executing a turn, how do you correct for the yaw resulting from use of ailerons?

A. By use of rudder in the direction of the roll. The actual turn is caused by the roll or bank. Rudder primarily corrects for yaw.

9. Q. When rolling into a turn, which aileron creates greater roll per degree of travel?

A. The raised aileron, because it moves up into an area of negative pressure and gives the effect of reverse camber, resulting in reduction of lift and drag. The down aileron moves into an area of positive pressure, resulting in more camber, increased lift, and materially increased drag. As a result the raised aileron causes most of the roll, and the down aileron assists the roll but causes most of the yaw.

10. Q. Do ailerons travel an equal distance up and down on the BT-13A?

A. No. Controls are designed so the raised aileron travels farther to effect greater roll without yaw and the down aileron travels less distance to avoid creating unnecessary yaw. This is called "differential aileron control." In the BT-13A ailerons travel up 25° and down 11½°.

11. Q. When is it possible to get a reverse reaction from ailerons?

A. This usually occurs when the airplane is in a stalled condition and the pilot tries to pick up a wing with the use of ailerons. This lowers the aileron on the "down-wing" side, greatly increasing the drag and further stalling the wing. There's both yaw and roll in the direction of the lowered aileron. This may force the airplane into a spin in that direction.

12. Q. Why are wrinkles in skin of the upper surface of the wings of little concern?

A. The main spar is designed to take all the bending load with aid only from the skin on the tension or bottom side. Since the skin on the top or compression side does not carry bending load, there is no cause for concern when wrinkles are observed during flight. The panels between spars and ribs of the Vultee wing are somewhat larger than in the usual wing, making the wrinkles more apparent to the eye.

13. Q. When should you use oil dilution control?

A. Only in extremely cold conditions when oil would congeal enough to make the engine difficult to start. At Basic schools the use of oil dilution is a function of the maintenance department. The pilot should not use oil dilution control until thoroughly instructed in its proper use.

14. Q. How do you test for carburetor ice?

A. If your carburetor mixture temperature is in the red, engine running rough (perhaps emitting black smoke from the exhaust), and you are losing rpms, suspect carburetor ice. To test, hold a given throttle setting and a given attitude of flight and apply full carburetor heat. Watch your tachometer. If ice is present, rpms will build up as the ice melts, but will fall off again when the ice is gone because of detonation caused by excessive heat. If there is an immediate decrease in rpms when heat is added, no ice is present and heat is causing loss in rpms. In that case, shut off the heat. If ice is present, adjust carburetor heat to get maximum rpms.

15. Q. When do you use the oil cooler shutter?

A. If the weather is very cold and your oil inlet temperature stays below operating limits, close the shutter enough to bring the temperature up. If it is very cold and the oil temperature goes sky high, the oil is probably congealing in the radiator preventing circulation. The shutter should be closed enough to stop this congealing.

# COMMON ERRORS

Common Errors are listed with each important maneuver in this manual. They help you recognize your own errors and analyze why you made them. Look for them in yourself and in your flying. Wherever you find them make the necessary corrections.

Following are some general shortcomings frequently found in students. Your instructor bases some of your grades on these points. Forewarned is forearmed!

## Common Errors in Attitude

1. Lack of military discipline.
2. Being disinterested, listless.
3. Disliking flying.
4. Non-aggressiveness, lack of initiative.
5. Not asking pertinent questions.
6. Asking unnecessary questions.
7. Being surly, resentful.
8. Fearing airplane, specific maneuver.
9. Wasting solo time.
10. Wasting spare ground time.
11. Cockiness.
12. Lacking self-reliance.
13. Fear of doing something wrong.
14. Polishing the apple.

## Common Errors in Judgment

1. Not thinking ahead of airplane.
2. Forgetting proper sequence of cockpit procedures.
3. Not retaining instruction.
4. Flying too close to other airplanes.
5. Making dangerously low turns.
6. Poor judgment on simulated forced landings.
7. Making slow decisions.
8. Recklessness.
9. Turning in front of other airplanes. Not allowing a margin for errors.
10. Fast taxiing.
11. Poor judgment of speed and distance.

## Common Errors in Progress

1. Slow understanding.
2. Poor retention of instruction.
3. Lack of progress after adequate instruction.

## Common Errors in Technique

1. Not coordinating. No feel of airplane.
2. Lack of division of attention.
3. Rough control movements, tense, jerky.
4. Making corrections too slowly.
5. Not correcting for torque.
6. Carelessness about details, cockpit procedures, control settings, etc.

# First Solo Flight

You are getting ready to solo. It's old stuff, the same kind of flying you've been doing. Prepare thoroughly, take your time, and your first solo flight in the Basic Trainer will go along as smooth as glass.

After you solo you'll spend a lot of time by yourself in the airplane. It's your own time and you will benefit from it in direct proportion to the way you use it. Remember that your country and your buddies are relying on your skill.

## Sophomore Stuff

Students admitted to pilot training are assumed to be adults with normal self-control and common sense. Occasionally a student will lose his head and yield to the temptation to do low flying, "buzzing," and other foolhardy antics. Reports of such violations, complete with the type and number of the plane, often beat the airplane back to the field. Punishment is swift and severe because such performances give a black eye to the Air Forces and to the home field.

The pilot who values his flying career will save the daredevil stuff for combat.

# *Pre-Solo* REQUIREMENTS

Here is a list of pre-solo requirements. You will be required to demonstrate a reasonable degree of proficiency and understanding of these operations and procedures before your instructor will let you solo.

1. Use of Cockpit Checklist. Blindfold Cockpit Test.
2. Altimeter Setting.
3. Use of Trim Tabs.
4. Use of Propeller Control.
5. Fuel Procedures and Changing Fuel Tanks.
6. Taxiing.
7. Use of Flap Control.
8. Take-Offs.
9. Torque Correction.
10. Climbing Turns.
11. Leveling Off.
12. Medium Turns.
13. Gliding Turns.
14. Clearing the Engine.
15. Traffic Pattern.
16. Landings.
17. Undershooting and Overshooting Procedure.
18. Clearing the Area.
19. Recovery from Stalls.
20. Recovery from Spins.
21. Forced Landings.
22. Radio.
23. Demonstration Stalls.
24. Three-Turn Spins.

## HOW TO LEARN FASTER

The more you can learn on the ground, the faster you'll learn in the air. Read what this manual has to say about your pre-solo requirements. It is a mistake to do only what you are told without learning why.

The fastest way to learn is to read up on the operations and procedures in advance. Then when your instructor explains them, you'll catch on more quickly and know what questions to ask. This will help you show faster progress in the air. Summarize in your mind "what to do," "why to do it," and "how to do it."

For the student's convenience, all pre-solo requirements are discussed in complete detail under separate headings in the pages that follow.

# BLINDFOLD COCKPIT TEST

Student_____ Date_____

Instructor_____ Grade_____

Student is considered proficient when he can place his hand on any of the controls or switches without hesitation within a period of 3 seconds. Sequence of order should be varied. Student must pass this test prior to solo.

Grade

1. Elevator Trim Tab Control . _____
2. Rudder Trim Tab Control . _____
3. Mixture Control . . . . _____
4. Throttle . . . . . . . _____
5. Flap Handle . . . . . _____
6. Propeller Control . . . . _____
7. Fuel Tank Selector Valve Control . . . . . . . _____
8. Wobble Pump Handle . . _____
9. Control Lock . . . . . _____
10. Rudder Pedal Adjustment Levers . . . . . . . _____
11. Primer . . . . . . . _____
12. Radio Interphone Switch . _____
13. CW-Voice-Tone Switch . . _____
14. Off-Auto-Manual Switch . _____
15. Receiving Tuning Unit . . _____
16. Volume Control Knob . . _____
17. Microphone . . . . . _____

Grade

18. High-Low Coil Switch . . _____
19. Pitot Heat Switch . . . _____
20. Parking Brake Handle . . _____
21. Landing Light Switch . . _____
22. Static Pressure Valve Control _____
23. Cockpit Light Switch . . . _____
24. Passing Light Switch . . . _____
25. Navigation Light Switch . . _____
26. Navigation Instrument Light Rheostat . . . . . . _____
27. Ignition Switch . . . . _____
28. Starter Switch . . . . . _____
29. Carburetor Heat Control . _____
30. Fuel Pressure Warning Light _____
31. Oil Cooler Shutter Control _____
32. Seat Adjustment Lever . . _____
33. Emergency Canopy Release _____

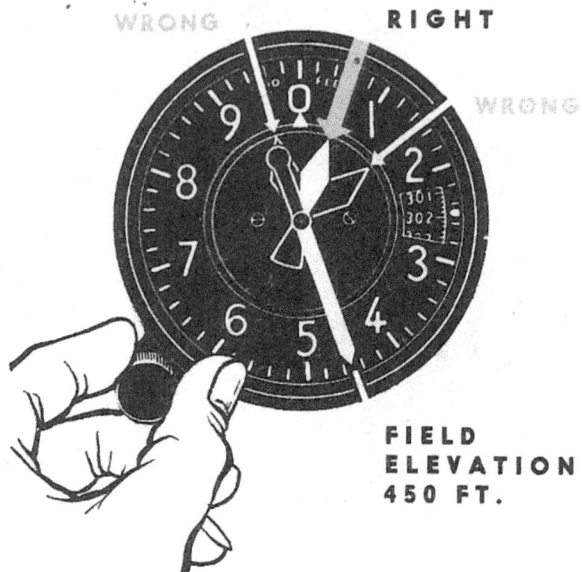

WRONG    RIGHT
WRONG

FIELD
ELEVATION
450 FT.

In the Basic Trainer, both elevator and rudder trim tabs can be adjusted from the cockpit during flight. You can immediately tell when the airplane is out of trim because of the excessive pressure on the stick or rudder. It is a favorite trick of some instructors to move the trim controls without warning to see if the student is wide awake enough to re-trim the airplane without being told. Here are pointers on the use of trim tabs:

Learn to zero the tabs by FEEL rather than by looking at them.

Always zero the tabs before take-off.

Re-trim the airplane for extensive glides and climbs as well as for level flight.

Correct the elevator trim setting quickly on an attempted landing that goes wrong before you give it full throttle to go around again.

## ALTIMETER SETTING

Students sometime wonder why they are accused of leveling off too high at cruising altitude, of flying traffic at the wrong altitude, or of making turns too low. This occurs when you forget to set the altimeter before taking off so it reads different from the instructor's altimeter.

If you aren't careful, it is very easy to set the altimeter below sea level or at 1,000 ft. above field elevation. This is confusing, will make your instructor think you have lost your mind, and can be exceedingly dangerous. Watch it.

Try turning your altimeter back and forth to incorrect settings so you know how it looks when it is set wrong.

For all student operations, set the altimeter at field elevation before starting the engine. Each successive student should check and re-set the altimeter if necessary.

## USE OF TRIM TABS

An airplane sidles through the air, fights the pilot, and tries to dive or climb when it's out of trim. A poorly trimmed airplane is harder to hold on course, increases pilot fatigue, and is harder to fly smoothly than one properly trimmed.

SIR SHE SEEMS AWFULLY TAIL HEAVY!

## PROPELLER CONTROL

Here are facts which will help you understand the proper use of the propeller control.

The blade angle of a fixed pitch propeller cannot be changed; an adjustable pitch propeller can be changed only on the ground, but the 2-position propeller on the Basic Airplane can be changed from the cockpit. This is a step toward the constant-speed propeller used in Advanced Training which, when set at a given rpm, automatically adjusts the pitch at various throttle settings to produce that rpm.

### High rpm (Low Pitch)

Propeller Control **FORWARD** (like full throttle) produces higher rpm, more power. Reason—the engine can turn up the propeller faster if it is taking smaller bites of air (Low Pitch) and can build up maximum thrust much more rapidly. Always use High rpm during take-offs and landings or you won't get maximum, quick power.

In thinking of the use of the Propeller Control, it is a good idea always to think in terms of "high rpm" or "low rpm." This saves time and avoids confusion.

### Low rpm (High Pitch)

Propeller Control BACK puts the propeller in Low rpm. Then the propeller is taking larger "bites" of air (high pitch), and gets more thrust out of a given amount of fuel. This is more practical for **cruising flight.**

Get this straight: **Propeller Control Forward** (High rpm) for Landings, Take-offs, Simulated Forced Landings — whenever you are likely to need lots of power quick.

### Use of Throttle

When the propeller control is moved back, throttle may be forward or back. But when the propeller control is moved forward, **throttle must be** back or the force of rotating counterweights (which hold the propeller in low rpm) will resist the oil pressure that changes propeller to high rpm.

**Note:** Oil pressure changes the propeller from Low rpm to High rpm and as this occurs a cylinder on the propeller hub moves out. If left in this position it will "weather," so it is necessary to draw this cylinder back into a sheltered position before stopping the engine. Before stopping the engine, move the propeller control back to Low rpm. This releases the oil pressure and the centrifugal force of counterweights will rotate the blades to the Low rpm position.

 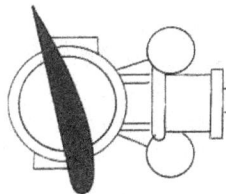 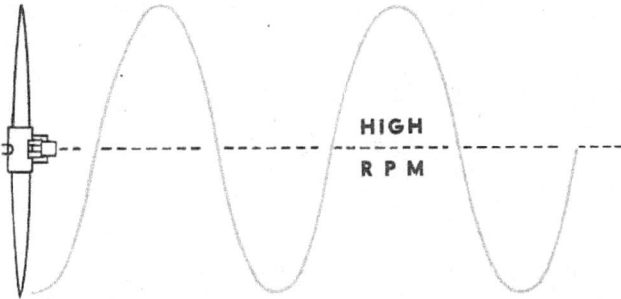

BLADE ANGLE

LOW PITCH

HIGH
R P M

**HIGH RPM FORWARD**

 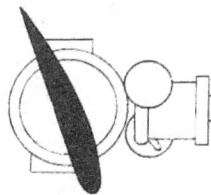 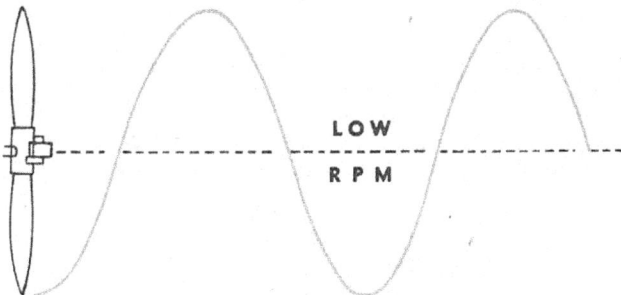

BLADE ANGLE

HIGH PITCH

LOW
R P M

**LOW RPM BACK**

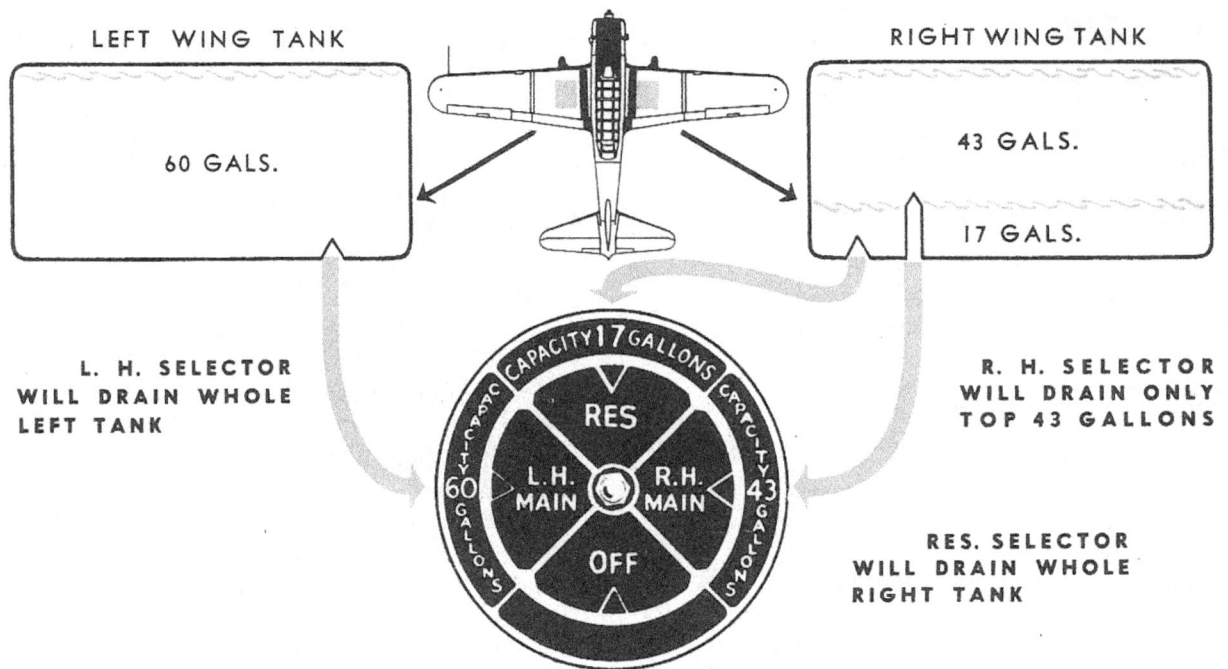

LEFT WING TANK

60 GALS.

RIGHT WING TANK

43 GALS.

17 GALS.

L. H. SELECTOR
WILL DRAIN WHOLE
LEFT TANK

R. H. SELECTOR
WILL DRAIN ONLY
TOP 43 GALLONS

RES. SELECTOR
WILL DRAIN WHOLE
RIGHT TANK

CAPACITY 17 GALLONS
RES
L.H. MAIN    R.H. MAIN
60 GALLONS    43 GALLONS
OFF

# FUEL PROCEDURES

The guy who can't watch his fuel gage during routine flights certainly won't remember it in a dog-fight with the enemy.

Beat yourself over the head with the simple truth that an airplane engine will not run without gasoline. Get gas conscious. Then you won't have to set a nice, shiny airplane down in somebody's pig-pen and walk home.

Take a couple of minutes and learn this fuel procedure.

### Before Take-Off

1. Check the fuel supply and check Forms 1 and 1A to see when the airplane was last serviced and how many hours it has been flown since. Figure that the BT-13A will burn about 25 gal. per hour on training flights.

2. Make all warm-ups and preflights on Reserve. Reason: There is no separate reserve tank in the Basic airplane. When on Right tank, fuel is drawn off through a standpipe in the Right tank. When on Reserve, fuel is drawn directly from the bottom of the Right tank. If there is water in the fuel, it will be at the bottom, and will be detected during starting and warm-up.

3. Change to the take-off tank before taxiing. When tanks are full, take off on the

Right main tank in the Vultee trainer and on the Left tank in the North American Trainer. Otherwise take off on the fullest tank.

### Proper Order for Using Fuel Tanks

Use tanks in a definite order. Here is the procedure recommended for the BT-13A:

1. If take-off is on the Right tank, fly until it is 10 gal. below the Left tank.

2. Switch to Left tank and fly until it is 10 gal. below the Right tank.

3. Switch to RESERVE. Continue to switch back and forth between Reserve and Left tank. Always keep these tanks within 10 gal. of each other.

### Changing Tanks

1. Change the selector valve pointer to the desired tank. Don't confuse the pointer with the handle. Make sure the valve **clicks** into position or the flow of fuel will be restricted.

2. Always use several easy strokes of the wobble pump immediately after changing tanks. This generates pressure to insure proper flow of fuel from the new tank and eliminates vapor lock or air locks in the line.

3. Keep an eye on the fuel pressure warning lamp. If it comes on, check to be sure the selector pointer is in position on a tank with gasoline in it. Then work the wobble pump and keep working it until the light goes out.

# TAXIING

If you want your instructor to scream himself bald-headed, turn in a taxiing accident that ruins three or four thousand dollars worth of airplane. Here's how to avoid taxiing accidents:

1. Place feet so that the rudder bar strikes the foot at the intersection of the heel and the sole of the shoe.

2. Taxi with the canopy open.

3. Start rolling before starting to turn so the steerable tailwheel will help the turn.

4. Taxi slowly, smoothly, and cautiously with a constant throttle setting at about the speed of a brisk walk.

5. Keep your head out of the cockpit and devote all your attention outside the airplane; look from side to side.

6. Keep your radio tuned to the tower so you can be called instantly, but do not use the microphone while taxiing. Keep your hand on the stick where it belongs.

7. "S" continuously in a pattern that will give a clear view of all that lies ahead.

8. Use the brakes sparingly, chiefly to stop the airplane or to help in making an unusually sharp turn.

## The Stick

Normally hold the stick in neutral or slightly back. When taxiing on a soft or rough field, the tail may have a tendency to bounce up. Hold the stick all the way back and the elevators will hold the tail down.

When taxiing downwind in a strong wind, hold the stick forward. This lowers the elevators, and the wind pressure against them holds the tail to the ground. If elevators are **up**, the wind can get under them and force the tail up.

If it is necessary to make a pivot turn without moving forward, hold the stick forward. This will raise some of the weight off the tailwheel so it will turn more freely to the swivel position. Use this procedure only when ABSOLUTELY NECESSARY.

Under certain conditions you may find it helpful to use ailerons when taxiing. Hold cross controls. For example, in a right turn you use right rudder and left aileron. The drag of the down aileron (right wing) helps you turn to the right. The up aileron is masked out by the leading edge of the wing.

WIND — STICK BACK

WIND — STICK FORWARD

# FLAPS

ANGLE OF GLIDE WITH
VARIOUS FLAP SETTINGS

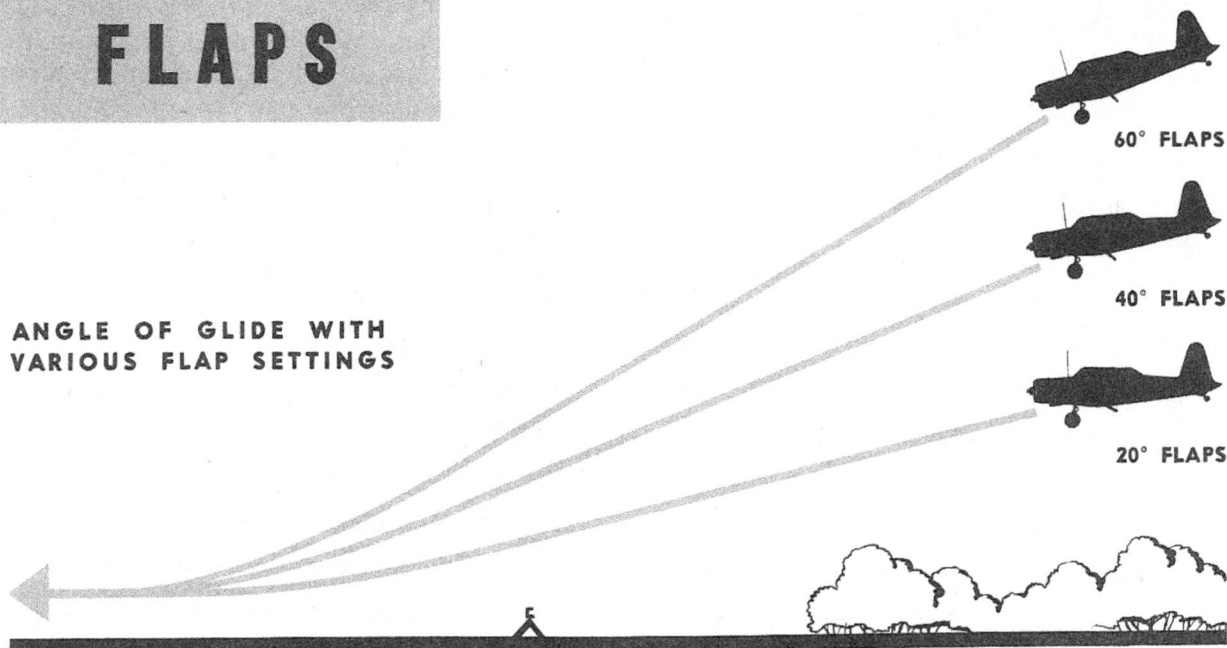

60° FLAPS

40° FLAPS

20° FLAPS

Lowering the flaps on an airplane is almost like putting a new wing on it. It's a different airplane and requires different treatment.

Lowering the flaps increases both the lift and the drag; it changes the angle of attack even though the airplane remains in the same attitude; and it decreases the stalling speed slightly. The effect of flaps varies from one type of airplane to another. The Vultee trainer, for example, has wings designed for higher efficiency at higher speeds, and flaps increase the lift and stability during all low-speed flying such as take-offs, climbs, and landings.

### Important

The correct use of flaps in flight is to steepen the gliding angle and not to decrease the gliding speed. Flaps must be used **properly.** Remember these things:

1. Never lower flaps at excessive speeds—never above 120 mph in Vultee trainer.

2. Keep a safe margin of speed above a stall and keep the airplane well nosed down.

3. Level off more abruptly with flaps, because you must make a greater change of attitude to get into position for a three-point landing.

4. If engine fails when flaps are down, **keep the flaps down.** If you raise them rapidly there is a sudden loss of lift.

5. Learn to locate and use the flap crank (without looking for it) and establish a given flap setting by a given number of turns of the crank. In the BT-13A one turn equals 2° of flaps.

6. Lower flaps on take-offs, climbs, glides, traffic pattern, simulated forced landing approaches, and stabilizer demonstration stalls (for Vultee Trainer).

7. Lower your flaps between the time you run up your engine and take-off. Otherwise, during taxiing or run-up, you may throw rocks through the flaps. This is not good.

## *Remember*

ONE TURN OF FLAP CRANK
EQUALS 2° OF FLAPS ON BT-13A

NEVER LOWER FLAPS IF
AIRSPEED IS OVER 120 MPH.

# TAKE-OFFS

Take-offs are easy in the BT-13A so make every one perfect. You are only going to fly this airplane for a couple of months and it doesn't pay to develop careless habits. Here is a list of take-off tips that will help you.

### Taxiing Out for Take-off

1. Follow the checklist procedure during starting, warm-up, and taxiing.
2. Keep tuned to the tower until well clear of traffic.
3. Taxi along a line at approximately right angles to the take-off path and keep the canopy open until clear of traffic.
4. Hold clear of the runway (or take-off path) at an angle of about 45° to see in both directions.
5. Check magnetos, and briefly run up the engine with full throttle to clear it and to be sure it is producing normal rpm of 1,950 to 2,000. **Caution!** Don't fly the airplane if the engine produces less than 1,850 rpm at full throttle. Something's wrong!

### Final Check

After engine run-up, crank down 20° of flaps. You should be all ready for take-off—but make a final check to be sure you haven't overlooked anything. Here is a sequence of letters summarizing the checklist items. Memorize them and use them as a quick check to make sure you have completed these procedures. Don't waste time repeating a detailed check.

C—**Controls** free.

I—**Instruments**—Temperature and pressures satisfactory. Altimeter set.

G—**Gas**—Supply adequate. Selector valve correctly set and mixture full rich.

F—**Flaps**—Down 10 turns, 20°.

T—**Trim**—Rudder and elevator trim tabs neutral.

P—**Propeller**—Forward in High rpm.

R—**Run-up**—Satisfactorily completed.

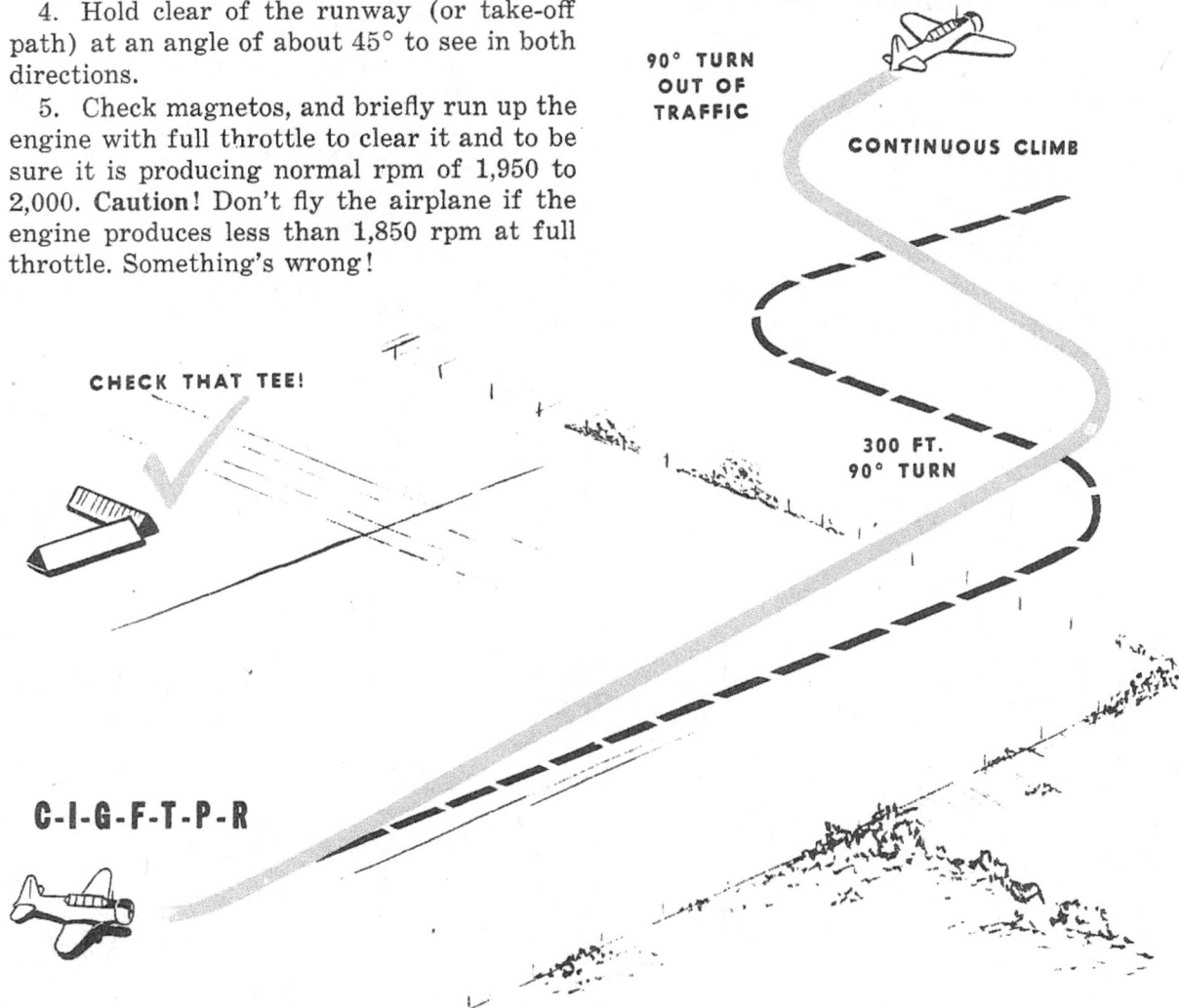

90° TURN OUT OF TRAFFIC

CONTINUOUS CLIMB

300 FT. 90° TURN

CHECK THAT TEE!

C-I-G-F-T-P-R

## The Take-Off Run

1. Take a good look in all directions, line up parallel with the Tee, and **take-off immediately.**

2. Open the throttle wide with a slow but steady movement. Jamming it open may cause the engine to misfire.

3. As you pick up speed keep the stick in neutral until the tail comes off the ground. Always keep it lower than in level flight.

4. As speed increases correct for torque by gradually increasing right rudder pressure. The easiest way to do this is simply to fix the nose on a point straight ahead and **hold it there.**

5. The airplane will lift itself off the ground at about 70 mph. Don't pull off directly into a climb because that's dangerous. Hold a minimum angle of climb until you build up an airspeed of 95 to 100 mph (slightly in excess of normal climbing speed), and hold this airspeed in traffic.

6. Adjust throttle to 2,100 rpm and, when out of traffic, establish a normal rate of climb.

## Wet Field Take-Off

1. On a soft field keep the tail within a few inches of the ground so you will lift into the air at minimum flying speed.

2. When off the ground, build up your airspeed before starting a climb. This is also the maximum performance take-off procedure.

## Turns After Take-Off

1. Your first turn will be a climbing turn at approximately 300 ft. above the ground **with traffic** (always beyond the boundary of the field). Look back in the direction of the turn and make definite 90° turns with a medium bank (about 40°).

2. After rolling out, hold straight ahead long enough to look around and make the second turn **away from traffic.** Continue to make climbing turns away from the field.

3. Always make definite turns. Don't ooze through them or you'll conceal your errors from yourself.

## Common Errors of Student

1. Trim tabs improperly set.
2. Fails to line up with Tee.
3. Throttle jammed forward.
4. Tail-high take-off.
5. Pulls airplane off the ground.
6. Fails to throttle back correctly.
7. Doesn't correct for torque or drift.
8. Angle of climb dangerously steep.
9. Starts turns too soon or too steep.
10. Doesn't look around before turning.

**NORMAL TAKE-OFF**

**WET FIELD TAKE-OFF**

# TORQUE

HIGH RPM—
LOW AIR SPEED—

TORQUE TENDS TO
TURN PLANE LEFT

POWER OFF—
RIGGING TENDS TO
TURN PLANE RIGHT

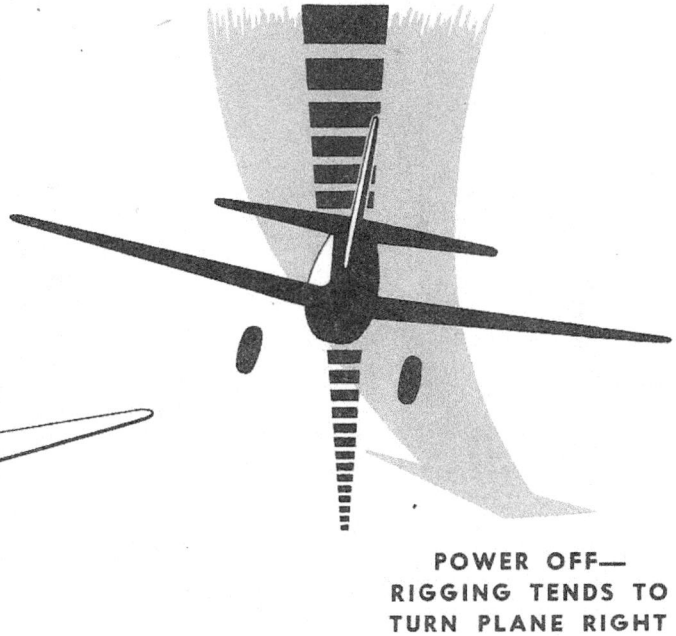

You will hear plenty about Torque as long as you fly the kind of airplanes being built today. The three most important things to know about Torque in the BT-13A are:

1. Torque tends to pull the nose of the airplane to the left during take-offs or when the airplane is in power-on climbing attitudes. The higher the rpms and the lower the airspeed, the more you notice the left pull. You have to use extra right rudder to counteract this pull.

2. The reason you don't notice much Torque effect in normal cruising flight is that the airplane is rigged to counteract it. (See Practical Questions and Answers on p. 20.)

3. Since Torque results from the action of the engine and propeller, it disappears in power-off maneuvers. But the airplane is still rigged for Torque so when power is off the nose tends to pull to the right. This is especially noticeable during glides and landings.

You don't have to know the technical facts about Torque as long as you can see what it does to the flight pattern you are trying to make and if you know how to counteract it.

But, if you want to know what some engineers say about Torque, here's the dope. Don't hope that you can read this as you read the comics. You'll have to **think** as you read.

Torque is the general name given to the forces that tend to make an airplane veer to the left during take-off and under certain conditions of flight. It is the result of a number of things—the Torque reaction set up by the propeller, the gyroscopic action of the propeller, the unsymmetrical loading of the propeller, and the action of the corkscrewing slipstream on the vertical tail surfaces. The order of importance of these causes is debatable. Here are further explanations of each:

## Torque Reaction Set Up By the Propeller

For every action there is always an equal and opposite reaction. The rotation of the propeller—a clockwise movement as viewed from the cockpit—tends to turn or roll the fuselage counter-clockwise. This pulls the airplane to the left.

You can understand this best by thinking of a rubber-band powered airplane model. Wind up the rubber-band for right-hand rotation of the propeller and then grasp the propeller and release the fuselage. The fuselage will rotate to the left. This same effect is present in a full-size airplane, except that the propeller, instead of being held still, is resisted by the air, and this resistance constantly tries to rotate the airplane opposite to the rotation of the propeller.

## GYROSCOPIC ACTION
## OF THE PROPELLER

The propeller of an airplane acts like a gyroscope and, like a gyroscope, it tends to precess if its axis is moved. If one axis of a spinning gyroscope is tilted, it will try to move (precess) about an axis at right angles to its original direction. You will notice this force particularly during take-off when you raise the tail quickly from the 3-point to a level flight attitude. The abrupt change of attitude moves the axis of the propeller, and precession causes the nose of the airplane to move toward the left. The amount that you feel the effect of the precession is directly related to the speed with which you raise the tail and thus change the position of the axis of the propeller.

## UNSYMMETRICAL LOADING
## OF THE PROPELLER

When an airplane is moving in a horizontal plane, but with a high angle of attack (a mushing condition) the bite of the downward-moving propeller blade in relation to the forward motion of the airplane is greater than the bite of the upward-moving blade. This causes a greater thrust on the downward-going blade which in turn tends to yaw the airplane to the left.

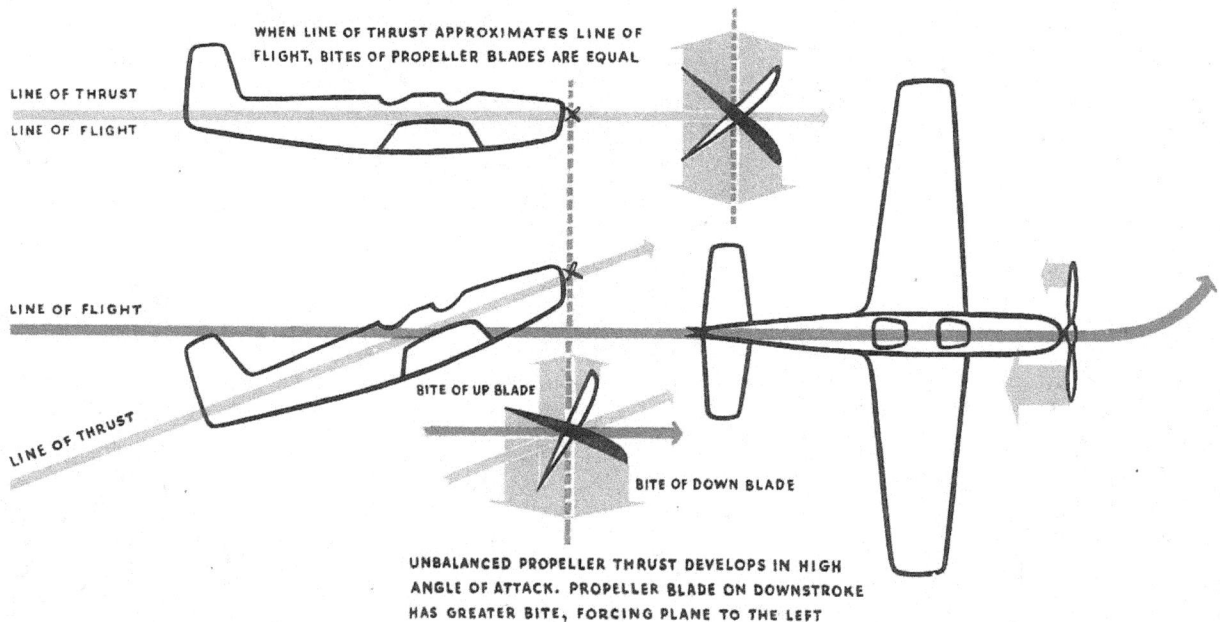

WHEN LINE OF THRUST APPROXIMATES LINE OF FLIGHT, BITES OF PROPELLER BLADES ARE EQUAL

LINE OF THRUST
LINE OF FLIGHT

LINE OF FLIGHT

LINE OF THRUST

BITE OF UP BLADE

BITE OF DOWN BLADE

UNBALANCED PROPELLER THRUST DEVELOPS IN HIGH ANGLE OF ATTACK. PROPELLER BLADE ON DOWNSTROKE HAS GREATER BITE, FORCING PLANE TO THE LEFT

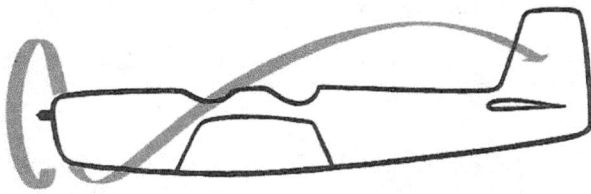

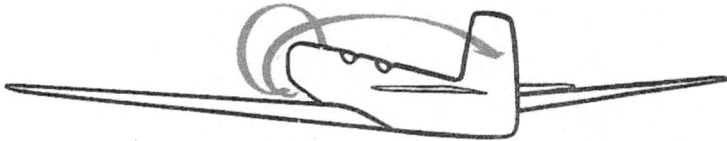

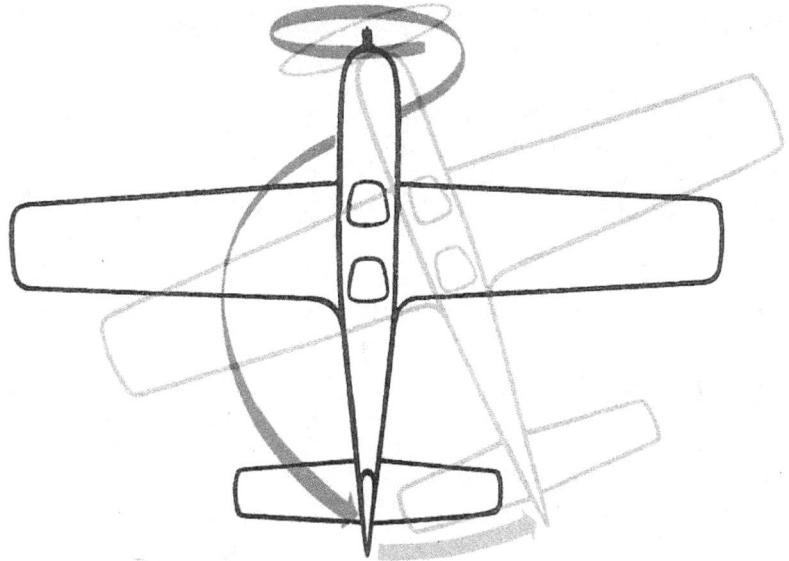

## ACTION OF THE
## CORKSCREWING SLIPSTREAM
## ON THE
## VERTICAL TAIL SURFACES

The high-speed rotation of an airplane propeller gives a corkscrewing rotation to the slipstream. The higher the rpm, the tighter the spiral of the slipstream. When this slipstream strikes the vertical tail surface, a yawing action is produced, tending to force the nose of the airplane to the left by pushing the tail towards the right. These facts apply to airplanes in which the propeller rotates clockwise as seen from the cockpit.

### LEAD WITH YOUR RIGHT

You can whip Torque. You've got a right foot and all you have to do is use it. When Torque shows up, push it aside with right rudder pressure.

Learn quickly to correct Torque and your instructor won't grind his teeth down to the gums nearly so fast.

# CLIMBING TURNS

Climbing turns teach you how to get maximum altitude safely in a minimum of time. As you turn, it is easy to look around and avoid all other traffic. Climbing turns also give you a chance to show your ability to coordinate controls and to hold a constant bank and a constant rate of climb.

Auxiliary Controls: Throttle set at 2,100 rpm; propeller in High rpm; flaps down 20° in Vultee trainer; no flaps in North American Trainer.

### Procedure

1. Check auxiliary controls in proper positions.

2. Establish the correct climbing attitude —nose above the horizon so that at 2,100 rpm the airspeed is about 90 mph. Notice where the horizon cuts across the nose of the airplane.

3. Establish and hold a bank of approximately 20° and use **enough rudder** to keep the nose moving in the turn at a constant rate of speed (without slipping or skidding). **Don't let the bank get gradually steeper.**

4. Correct for torque. Notice that it takes definite right rudder pressure to establish and hold a climbing turn to the right but very little or no left rudder pressure in climbing turns to the left. In fact, after your climbing turn to the left is established, you may have to use a little right rudder. Failure to allow for torque is the most common student error. Maintain a constant rate of turn by keeping the nose moving steadily along the horizon.

5. Use a reference line so you make definite 90° turns. At first roll out into a climb straight ahead after each turn. Later you will practice both 90° and 180° turns, rolling from one directly into another.

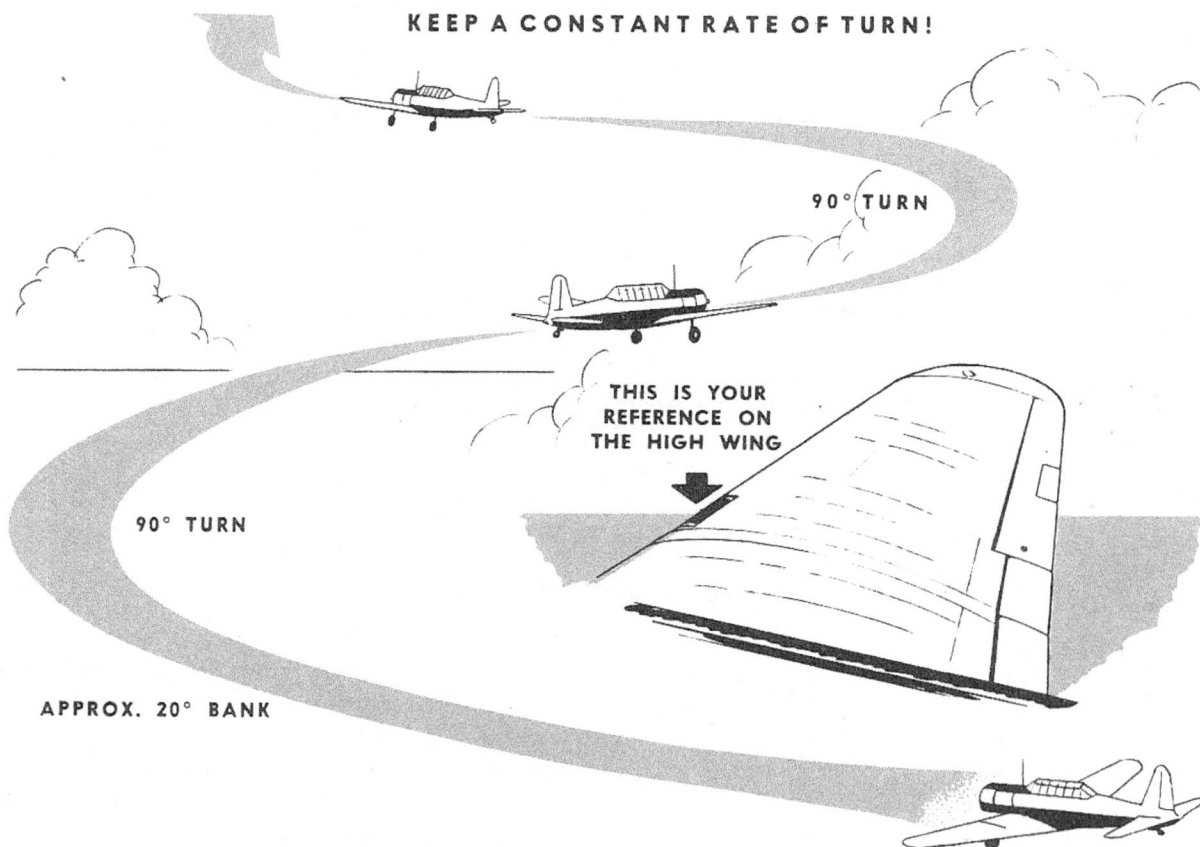

KEEP A CONSTANT RATE OF TURN!

90° TURN

THIS IS YOUR REFERENCE ON THE HIGH WING

90° TURN

APPROX. 20° BANK

**NOTE**

Keep rudder trim tab in cruising position during climbing turns until you have completed 30 to 35 hours of flying. After that, trim the rudder tab to correct for torque in climbing turns.

# Leveling Off

In Basic Training, Leveling Off is a precision operation that gives you a preview of the step-by-step procedures important in handling larger aircraft. Accuracy is what you are shooting for. Think ahead of the airplane and you'll hit your altitude on the nose every time.

1. Exceed the desired altitude by about 150 to 200 ft.
2. Move the Propeller Control back to Low rpm, lower the nose into a shallow dive, and roll up the flaps as you dive.
3. Level off at the desired altitude and wait, before adjusting throttle to cruising rpm, until the engine has a chance to build up speed. Usually very little, if any, throttle adjustment will be required.
4. Trim the airplane for cruising flight.

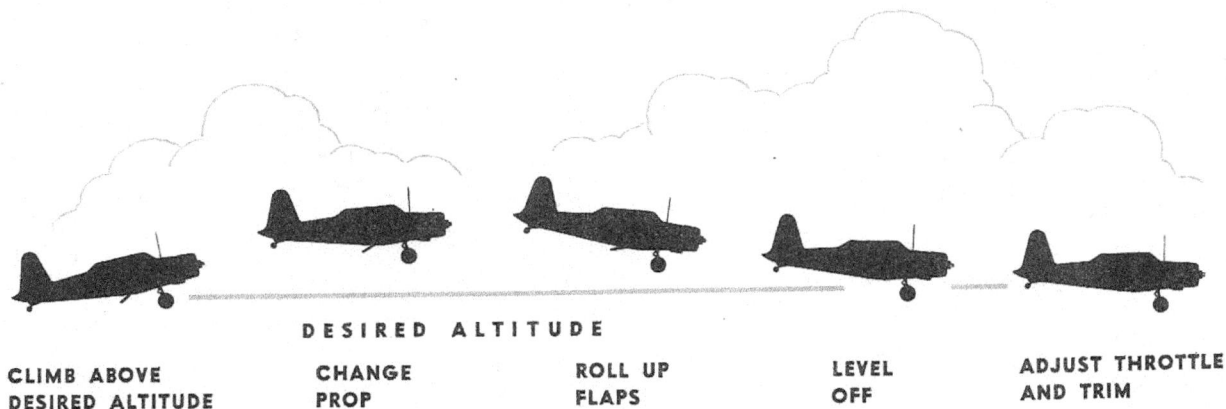

DESIRED ALTITUDE

CLIMB ABOVE DESIRED ALTITUDE     CHANGE PROP     ROLL UP FLAPS     LEVEL OFF     ADJUST THROTTLE AND TRIM

# MEDIUM TURNS

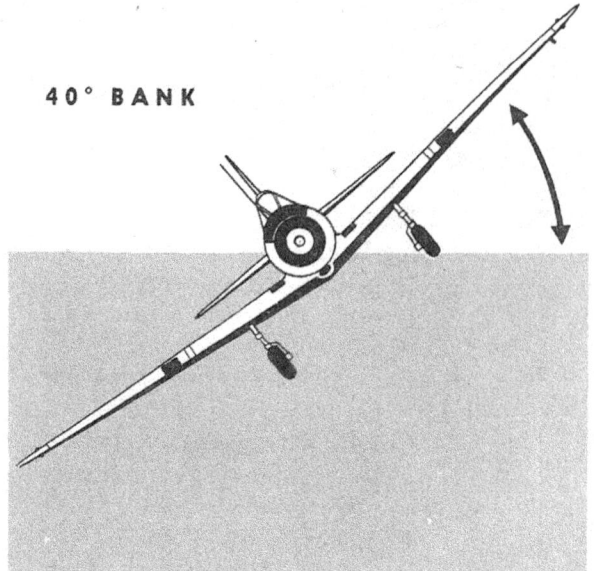

This is one of the first things you will practice. The more quickly you demonstrate smoothness, precision, and good control, the more quickly you'll be allowed to do more complicated maneuvers.

Remember that there is no room in the sky for a pilot with a stiff neck. Combat pilots report that the habit of looking around is as vital as the ability to shoot . . . and is the only thing that will prevent surprise in enemy skies. Always look around before you turn.

**Auxiliary Controls:** In cruising position.

**Important Points:** Good Medium Turns require a smooth roll into a 40° angle of bank, without slipping or skidding, and a **constant rate of turn** through 90° to 180°.

Line up with a road, fence, or other reference point and make turns exactly 90° or 180°. The most difficult part of turns is the precision roll-out in which the wings return to level just as the turn is completed, the nose on a point straight ahead. You must anticipate the roll-out and time it with great care to roll out level at exactly the right point. Hesitate in level flight after each turn until you have mastered the roll-out. Then practice rolling from one bank into another.

Keep the nose moving steadily along the horizon to achieve a constant rate of turn without slipping or skidding. In a closed cockpit you must **sit relaxed in the center of the seat** and feel the slip or skid.

If the airplane is slipping in a left turn, for example, you will feel yourself sliding toward the inside of the turn. If the airplane is skidding, your body will tend to move or slide toward the outside of the turn. Sit back in your seat, hold the stick lightly, and relax your muscles. That's the only way to develop a smooth touch.

## Common Errors of Student

1. Doesn't look around before starting turn.
2. Over-controls with the ailerons.
3. Slips or skids.
4. Fails to maintain a constant bank or a constant rate of turn.
5. Is tense and tightens up on the controls.
6. Fails to make definite 90° or 180° turns.
7. Starts roll-out too soon or too late.

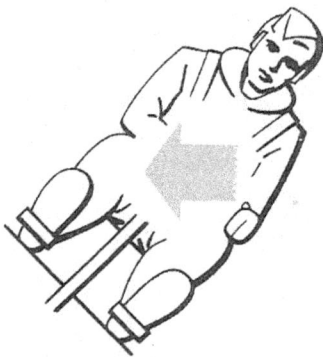

**SKID**

**COORDINATED**

**SLIP**

# GLIDING TURNS

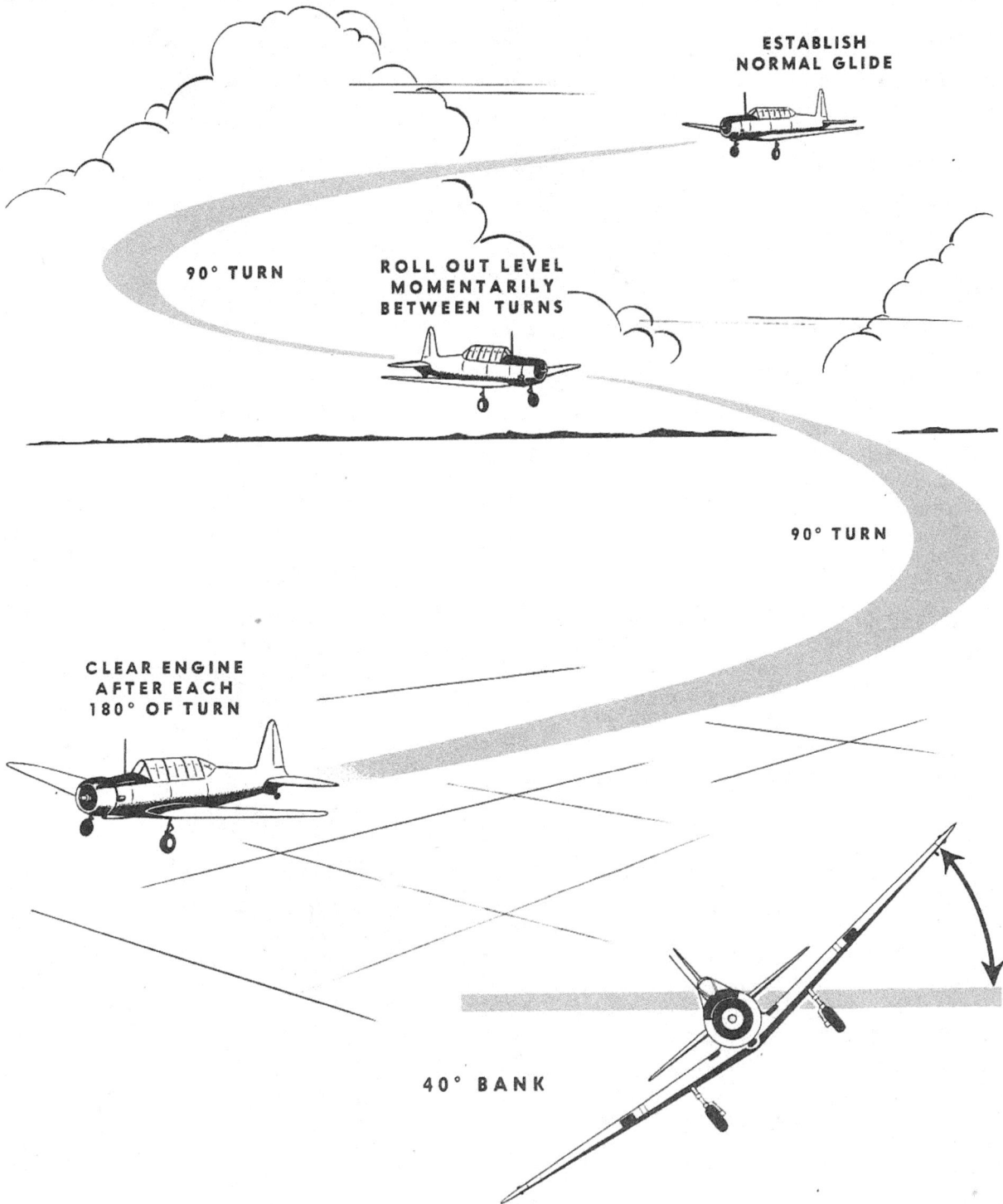

ESTABLISH
NORMAL GLIDE

90° TURN

ROLL OUT LEVEL
MOMENTARILY
BETWEEN TURNS

90° TURN

CLEAR ENGINE
AFTER EACH
180° OF TURN

40° BANK

Smooth Gliding Turns are necessary to fly properly in traffic, to line up accurately for runway landings, and to execute simulated forced landings properly.

### Auxiliary Controls

The first step in making Gliding Turns is to set the controls properly for a normal glide:

1. Cut the throttle.
2. Move propeller control forward to High rpm.
3. Hold the airplane in level flight until the airspeed drops below 120 mph and then lower 20° of flaps (on Vultee Trainer).
4. Dissipate airspeed to about 90 mph and establish a normal glide to maintain that airspeed.
5. Trim the airplane.

Notice the position of the nose in relation to the horizon and notice the sound and feel of the airplane. Always hold the glide by feel and by attitude—not by looking at the airspeed indicator. Keep your head out of the cockpit.

### How to Turn

Line up on a road or other reference line, look around always, and roll smoothly from a straight ahead glide into a 40° angle of bank. You can control the gliding speed by holding the nose at a constant angle below the horizon.

The nose should move around below the horizon at the same steady rate of speed whether the turn is to the left or the right. Students tend to slip in Gliding Turns to the left because with throttle retarded the torque rigging tends to swing the nose to the right. This calls for extra left rudder pressure in all glides. Avoid the common tendency to **use too much aileron** and **not enough rudder pressure** when rolling in and out of turns. This is not the same airplane you used to fly.

Practice the same definite 90° Gliding Turns that you will use later in traffic, and roll out into the glide straight ahead after each turn. Always clear the engine after 180° of turn or more often if weather requires it.

Remember that good Gliding Turns are the first step toward good landings and that you won't solo until you can make safe, coordinated Gliding Turns.

### Common Errors of Student

1. Fails to correct for the absence of torque.
2. Inability to feel the glide.
3. Fails to hold a constant angle of glide or bank.
4. Fails to turn through 90°.
5. Too much aileron pressure and not enough rudder.
6. Doesn't clear engine at the right time or in the proper manner.
7. Can't maintain a constant rate of turn.
8. Doesn't look around before turning.

## Clearing the Engine

Clear the engine in this airplane after 180° of turn or more often if necessary. Why? Because with throttle retarded, the engine is cooling rapidly. Gas vapors are condensing and may foul the plugs unless properly cleared. Cylinder head temperature should never get below 100° C. In cold or damp weather it may be necessary to clear the engine after every 90° of turn. Show your instructor you can use good judgment.

### How to Use the Throttle

Don't use short bursts of power because you'll overload the engine with a rich, unvaporized mixture. The proper way is to advance the throttle slowly and smoothly until you reach 2,000 rpm. As soon as the engine takes hold, raise the nose to avoid building up too much speed. Run the engine long enough to be sure it's clear, but never allow rpm to exceed the indicated engine limits.

When you cut the throttle again, hold the airplane in level flight until you lose excess speed, and then lower the nose again to normal gliding attitude.

# TRAFFIC PATTERNS

Sloppy flying and serious accidents often result from improper understanding of Tee settings and Traffic Patterns. You are at a new field, so dig in and learn the traffic patterns as fast as possible. It doesn't cost a cent to ask questions.

## Tee Settings

All Basic Schools have standard Tee settings, not exceeding eight in number. As nearly as possible one Tee setting conforms to the prevailing wind. The others are developed around it, i.e., 45°, 90°, and 180° to it, and are numbered to correspond to the magnetic heading used, for example, No. 7 is at 70°, No. 36 is at 360°, etc.

To check your knowledge, sit down and draw your own rough chart of the field. Lay out a Tee and move it around in various settings. Check with other students to see if you all agree on the Tee settings and patterns.

## Traffic Tips

1. To determine traffic, fly over the field at 1,500 ft. above the ground to see the Tee and observe other airplanes.

2. Change to High rpm at least 1,000 ft. above the ground and use a power let-down to traffic altitude at least one-half mile before entering the downwind leg.

3. Fly traffic at 700 ft. above the ground and follow the Traffic Pattern **always.**

4. Make all turns medium banks (approximately 40° of bank) through 90° of turn. If you are going to have to establish a crab to correct for drift, estimate the crab and complete the turn so that you will have the desired amount of crab when you roll out. Use a definite bank and a **definite** roll-out to show other airplanes what you are doing.

5. Look around and KEEP LOOKING. Maintain proper spacing and don't land **too close** to other airplanes.

6. Stay **above 1,500 ft.** above the ground when near the home or auxiliary fields and when not flying in traffic.

7. Traffic violations will not be tolerated at **any field.** Local conditions at your station may require changes from the traffic regulations set forth in this manual. It is your job to **know** the traffic rules at your field and obey them. Ignorance is no excuse!

★ LOOK AROUND IN TRAFFIC!

★ KEEP THAT BASE LEG IN!

# PATTERN FOR A 1-WAY FIELD

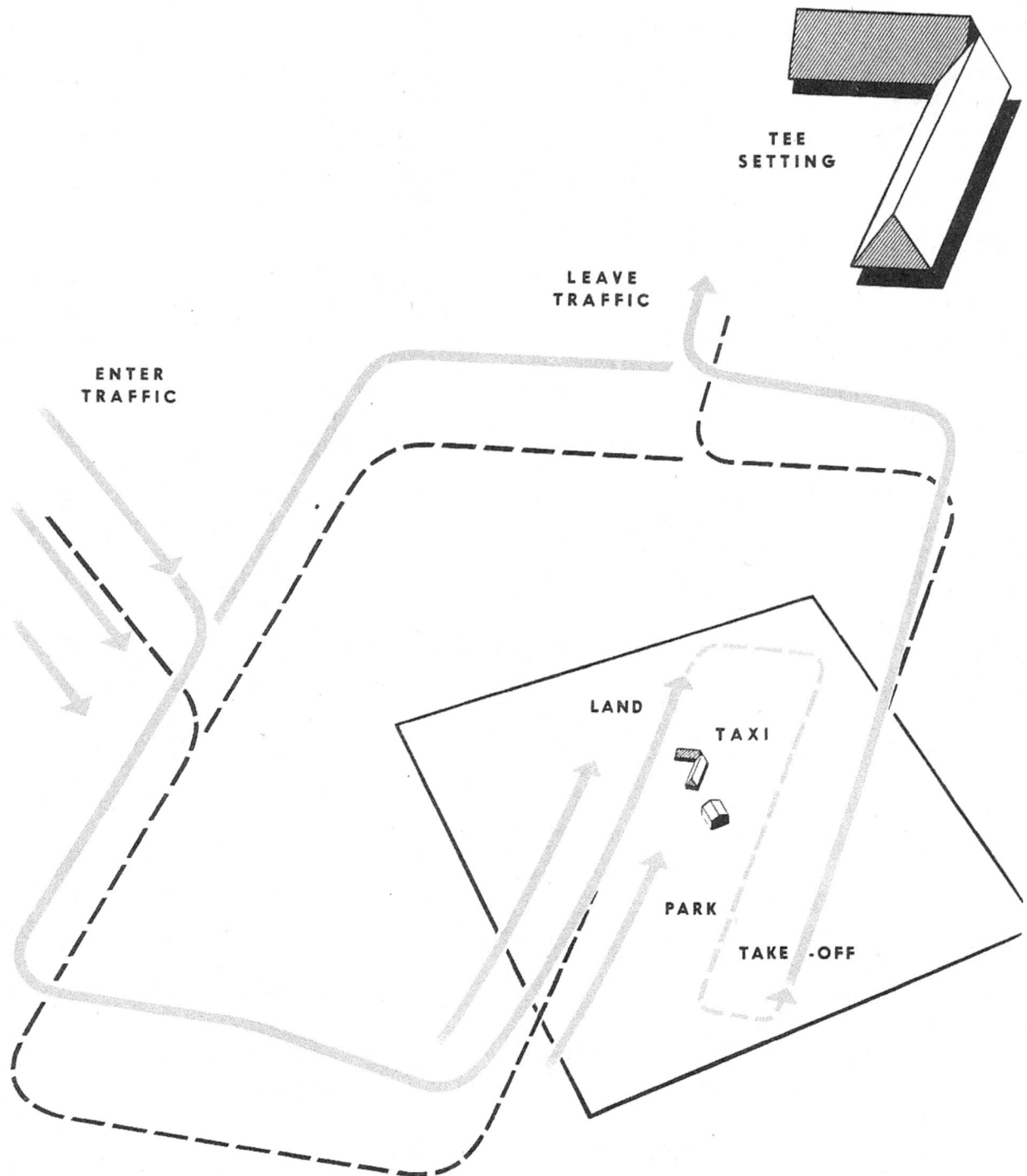

TEE
SETTING

LEAVE
TRAFFIC

ENTER
TRAFFIC

LAND

TAXI

PARK

TAKE-OFF

# PATTERN FOR A 2-WAY FIELD

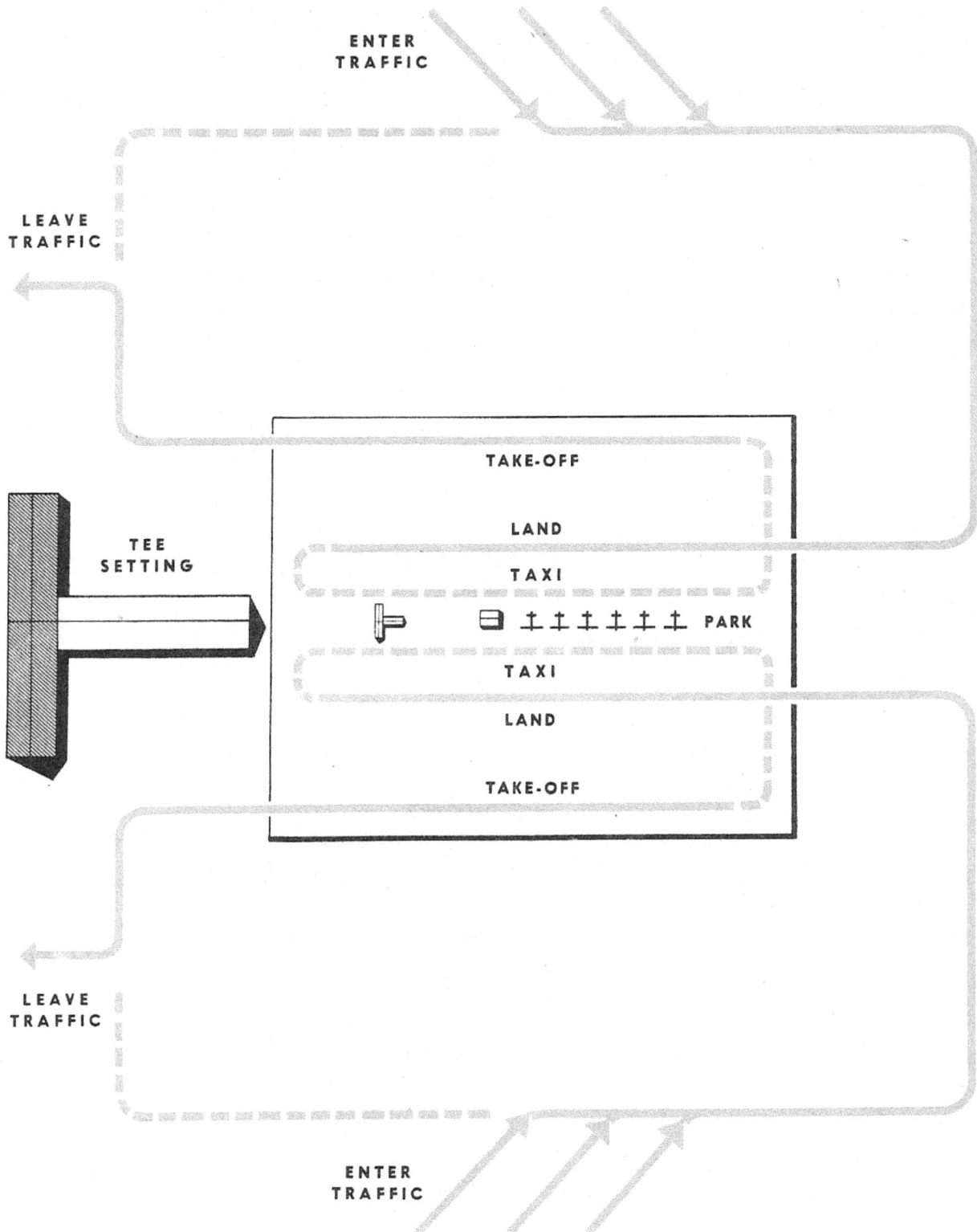

ENTER
TRAFFIC

LEAVE
TRAFFIC

TEE
SETTING

TAKE-OFF

LAND

TAXI

PARK

TAXI

LAND

TAKE-OFF

LEAVE
TRAFFIC

ENTER
TRAFFIC

# PATTERN FOR A 2-WAY FIELD, ONE SIDE CLOSED

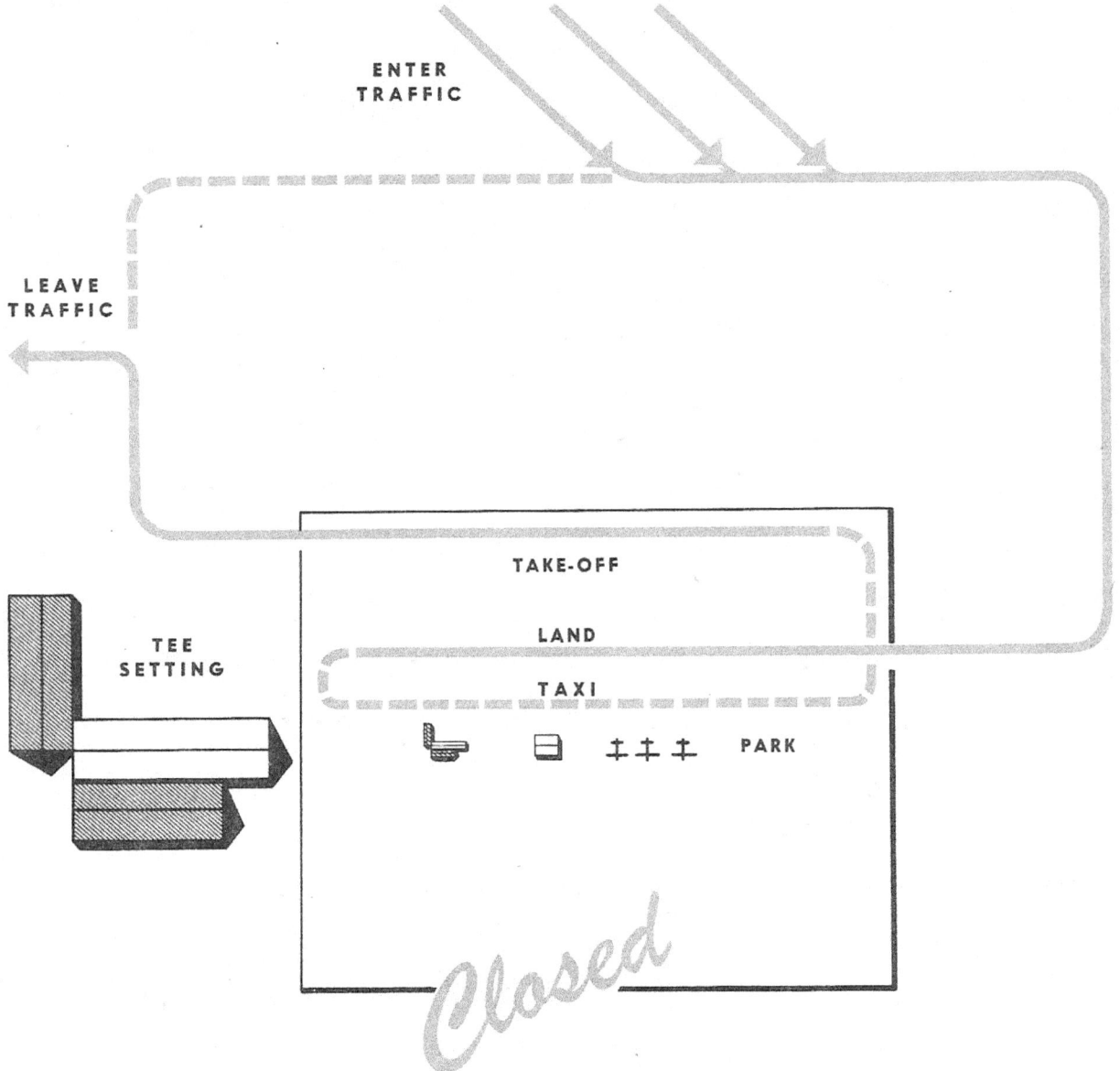

ENTER
TRAFFIC

LEAVE
TRAFFIC

TEE
SETTING

TAKE-OFF

LAND

TAXI

PARK

Closed

# Landings

Merely landing the Basic Airplane is not difficult. But consistent, precision 3-point landings require concentrated practice.

Students tend to concentrate too much, too soon, on the landing itself. Don't make this mistake. It will result in a poor traffic pattern, erratic gliding turns, and **uncoordinated** use of controls. You will progress much faster if you will follow this standard landing procedure:

## Approaching Traffic

1. Tune to the tower frequency and change to the fullest tank before you let down. Plan your let-down so that when you reach 1,000 ft. you can head at an angle of 45° to the downwind leg.

2. Change to High rpm and open your canopy at least 1,000 ft. above the ground. Then reduce your airspeed below 120 mph, roll down 20° of flaps, and bring the airplane to traffic altitude at least one-half mile before entering the downwind leg.

3. Re-trim the airplane, establish an airspeed of 105 to 110 mph, and enter anywhere along the last half of the downwind leg.

4. Fly traffic at an airspeed of 105 to 110 mph or 2,000 rpm depending on your local procedure.

If operations are timed as outlined above, you will be free to concentrate all your attention on an accurate approach and on correct turns. Make definite 90° medium turns.

## On the Base Leg

Make a final check just after completing the turn into the base leg to be sure you have completed the checklist procedures. Shout out the check letters so your instructor can hear you:

G—Gas—Fullest Gas Tank is being used.

M—Mixture—Mixture at Full Rich.

P—Propeller—Propeller is in High rpm.

Remember the spot on the base leg where you cut the throttle (Key Point) so you will be able to make corrections on the next landing. The turn into the approach leg should be made at about 500 ft. above the ground— never below 300 ft. Be careful not to cross controls. This is Dangerous!

## Final Approach

After turning on the final approach, roll down 20° more flaps and lower the nose just enough to maintain safe gliding speed. Throughout the landing, relax in the center of the cockpit with your eyes shifting to judge the landing more accurately. Be sure you are not going to land directly behind or too near another airplane. It's no disgrace to go around again.

Start to break your glide slowly and smoothly at 30 to 50 ft. above the ground. Continue to round out your glide gradually so that the airplane will be in landing attitude as it reaches the ground. Avoid sudden or jerky back pressure. If you wait too long to round out the glide, you will have excess speed when you level off and will float on and on down the field. This interferes with accuracy and makes it hard to complete a good 3-point landing.

## Leveling Off Too High

If you see you have leveled off too high, relax the back pressure slightly to bring the airplane closer to the ground and then re-establish a landing attitude. If a wing drops, or the airplane starts to stall, use the throttle and rudder immediately to regain control. Remember all you learned about stalls, the Characteristic Stall in particular.

## Landing Wheels First

If you land wheels-first, don't come back on the stick, or the airplane will zoom up again and may stall and drop in.

Hold the stick where it is when you hit the ground and you won't get in serious trouble. A very slight amount of forward pressure on the stick, just as you contact the ground, will help prevent a bounce. This helps to hold your wheels on the ground as in an airliner landing. Keep the nose on a point straight ahead and the tail will settle when the airplane slows down.

If you come in wheels-first and bounce high into a semi-stalled condition, apply throttle as necessary to re-establish a normal landing attitude. Keep flying the airplane.

## The Landing Roll

Keep the stick all the way back until the airplane stops rolling, and hold the nose steadily on a point straight ahead. Raise your feet to a braking position after one-third of the Landing Roll, and use brakes sparingly except to prevent ground loops and collisions. In emergencies use more brakes in the early part of the Landing Roll, when elevators will hold the tail down, and less brakes as elevators become less effective.

Continue to fly the airplane until it stops rolling and always look behind before making a turn. Roll up the flaps and put trim in neutral after the Landing Roll and before you start taxiing. Most ground loops occur because the pilot starts doing chores in the cockpit before he has completed his Landing Roll.

## Accuracy

A more complete discussion of how to achieve accuracy in landing is given under "90° Accuracy Stages," p. 89. Read this right now. It will help you perfect your landings that much faster and "Time's a-wastin'." **Make every landing an accurate one.**

## Common Errors of Student

1. Fails to establish proper glides.
2. Glides too fast or dangerously slow.
3. Undershoots or overshoots.
4. Lands Cross-Tee.
5. Makes wheels-first or tail-first landings.
6. Bounces and ignores the throttle.
7. Stops flying before the airplane stops rolling.
8. Lands too close to other airplanes.
9. Doesn't **Look Around.**

## Undershooting

1. When undershooting, don't wait! Immediately use enough throttle to bring the airplane on into the field.
2. Lift the nose enough to prevent too much build-up of speed.
3. Then, when safely near the field, re-establish a normal glide and land in the usual manner.

## Overshooting

1. If you use additional flaps early enough, it will help to prevent overshooting.
2. If there is any doubt, give it full throttle and go around. Don't take a chance.
3. **If you decide to go around, hold the nose down** . . . and **quickly** adjust the elevator trim tab to avoid a stabilizer stall.
4. Don't pull up into a steep climb. Keep your climb shallow until the engine has a chance to build up rpm and forward speed.
5. After you are well clear of all obstacles, slowly roll up part of the flaps but keep 20° down for greater climbing efficiency (on Vultee Trainer).
6. Reduce the throttle to keep from exceeding maximum rpm.

# LANDING PROCEDURE

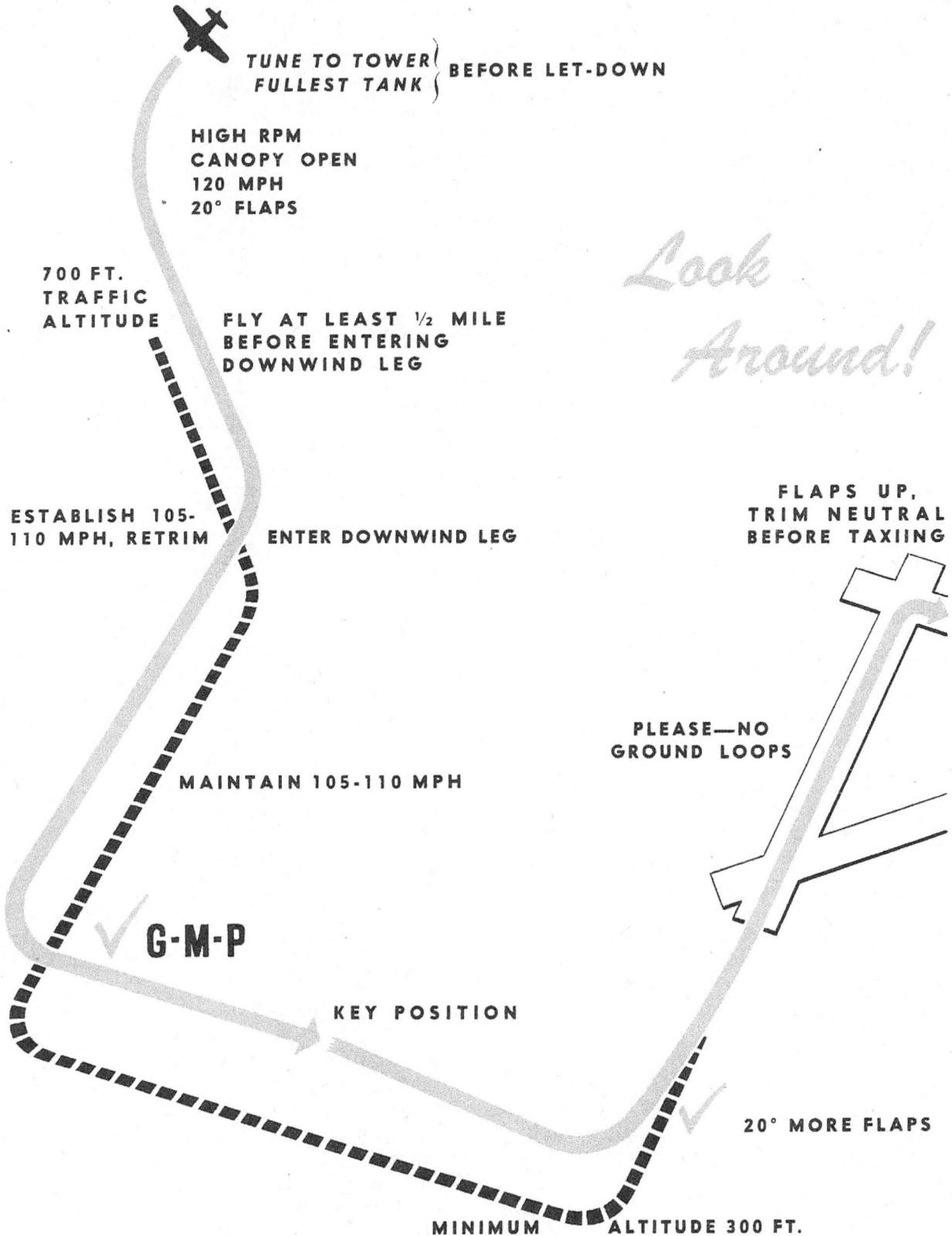

*TUNE TO TOWER*
*FULLEST TANK* ⟩ BEFORE LET-DOWN

HIGH RPM
CANOPY OPEN
120 MPH
20° FLAPS

700 FT.
TRAFFIC
ALTITUDE

FLY AT LEAST ½ MILE
BEFORE ENTERING
DOWNWIND LEG

*Look
Around!*

ESTABLISH 105-
110 MPH, RETRIM    ENTER DOWNWIND LEG

FLAPS UP,
TRIM NEUTRAL
BEFORE TAXIING

MAINTAIN 105-110 MPH

PLEASE—NO
GROUND LOOPS

✓ G-M-P

KEY POSITION

20° MORE FLAPS

MINIMUM    ALTITUDE 300 FT.

# CLEARING THE AREA

There is always danger of mid-air collisions. Always clear the area with special care before maneuvers which involve sudden gain or loss of altitude or change of direction.

To Clear the Area, make enough turns to observe all other aircraft in the vicinity. This will vary with the amount of traffic and with the nature of the maneuver to be performed. Remember these things:

Look before you turn or climb or dive, and fly in the area you have just cleared.

Begin the maneuver immediately after clearing the area.

Always make allowances for a muffed maneuver.

*Take a Good Look*

## Stalls

The Basic airplane has excellent stall characteristics for its purpose. It can be stalled fairly easily and at the same time will recover readily. There are many kinds of stalls and various factors affect the reactions of the airplane when the stall occurs. The most important of these are the power setting, the attitude of the airplane, the position and use of controls, and the wing loading.

### Why Stalls Are Practiced

Stalls are practiced for two important reasons: first, so you'll know how to recover if a stall occurs unexpectedly; second, because a pilot must understand stalls to make a good 3-point landing, to execute a maximum performance climbing turn, to make hurdle landings, or to do a good chandelle or other advanced maneuvers. You've got to **Know Your Stalls** to get maximum performance out of an airplane in combat. That's why so much time and emphasis are given to stalls in Basic Training.

### Three Things to Learn

There are three key things to learn about stalls:

1. How to recognize an approaching stall.
2. How to recognize the stall itself.
3. How to recover from various types of stalls.

You can **See**, **Hear**, and **Feel** a Stall approaching in the Basic airplane. Controls begin to loosen up, the engine labors harder and harder, there is a sinking, mushy feeling, and you can see the stalling attitude. Then the stall itself—a slight buffeting of the wings, vibration of the fuselage, and the nose or a wing drops. It's time for recovery—the most important part of all stall work.

The difference between a good and a sloppy recovery is hundreds of feet of altitude—the difference between safety and a crash.

### Entries Into Stalls

Enter all stalls at 4,000 ft. above the ground or higher. Clear the area thoroughly. You can lose considerable altitude in a stall maneuver.

Your instructor will emphasize the importance of precision entries into stalls because he knows you will learn just as much from the entry as from the stall itself. The entry gives you a chance to show that you can establish and hold a given attitude of flight, constantly correcting for decreasing airspeed and increasing torque. Learn the specified entries and fly them accurately.

# Checklist of Stalls

## CURRICULUM STALLS

Characteristic Stall
(Power Off)

Rudder Controlled Stall
(Power On)

Normal Recovery Stalls
(Power On)

Normal Recovery Stalls
(Power Off)

In the approach to a stall,
establish the same attitude
as in Normal Recovery Stalls,
(Power On).

## STALLING ATTITUDE

Straight Ahead,
Landing Attitude

Straight Ahead,
50° Climb

Straight Ahead,
40° Climb

Right and Left,
40° Climb, 20° Bank

Straight Ahead,
Landing Attitude

Right and Left,
nose slightly above
horizon, 40° bank

Same as Normal Recovery Stalls, Power On

ABOVE ARE THE STALLS THAT STUDENTS WILL PRACTICE BOTH
DUAL AND SOLO UNTIL PROFICIENT

## DEMONSTRATION STALLS (DUAL ONLY)

Secondary Stall—Power On
(Straight Ahead)

Stabilizer Stall—Power On
(Straight Ahead)

Excessive Back Stick Stalls—Power On
(Right and Left)

Excessive Top and Bottom Rudder Stalls—Power On
(Right and Left)

Cross Control Stall—Power Off
(Right and Left)

## DEMONSTRATION STALLS WILL NOT BE PRACTICED SOLO!

# Notes on the AERODYNAMICS OF STALLS

## LIFT AND DRAG

**Normal Angle Of Attack**

● LEAST DRAG
● NORMAL LIFT

**Climbing Angle Of Attack**

● MORE DRAG
● MOST LIFT

**"CRITICAL" or Stalling Angle Of Attack**

● MOST DRAG
● LEAST LIFT
(Burble Point)

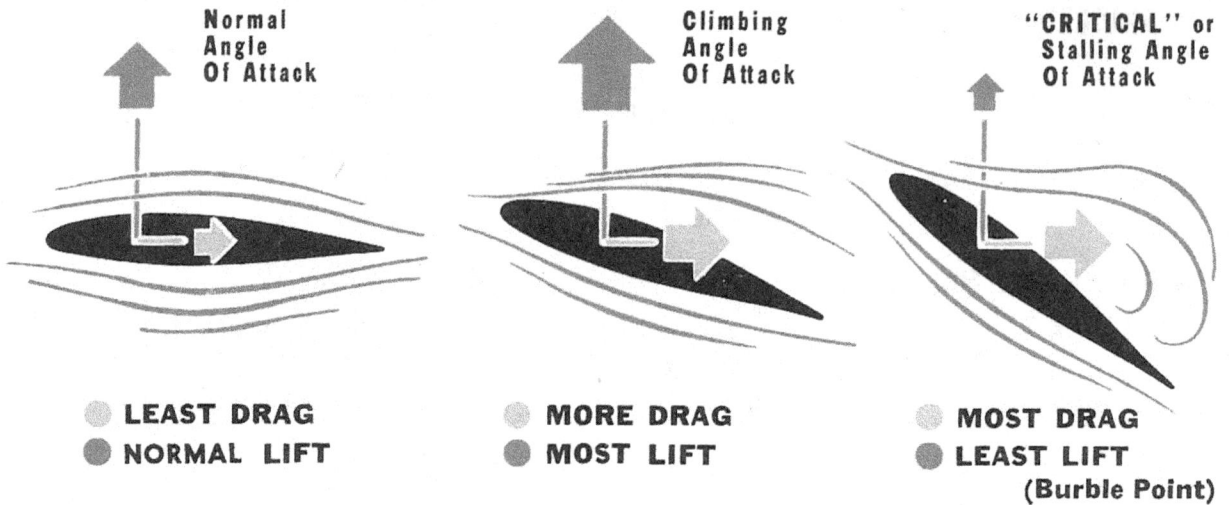

## HIGH SPEED STALL

**Sudden Increase In Angle of Attack**

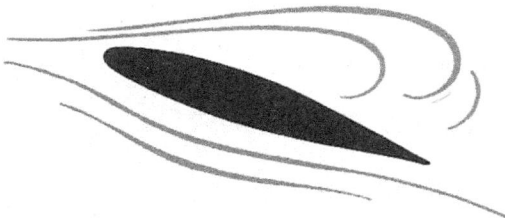

**Normal Level Flight**

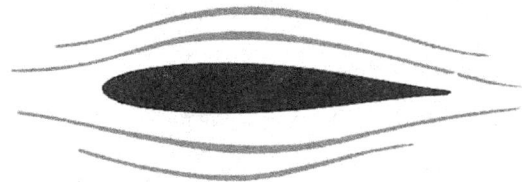

**Burble Point Reached Immediately**

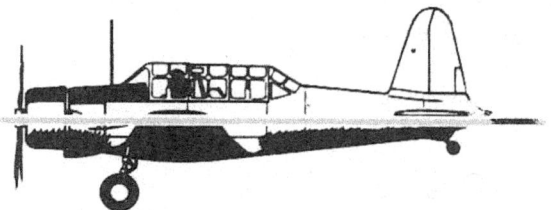

HORIZONTAL FLIGHT PATH

Sudden Back Pressure on Controls.
Inertia Carries Plane In Same
Horizontal Flight Path.

# STALL IN A TURN

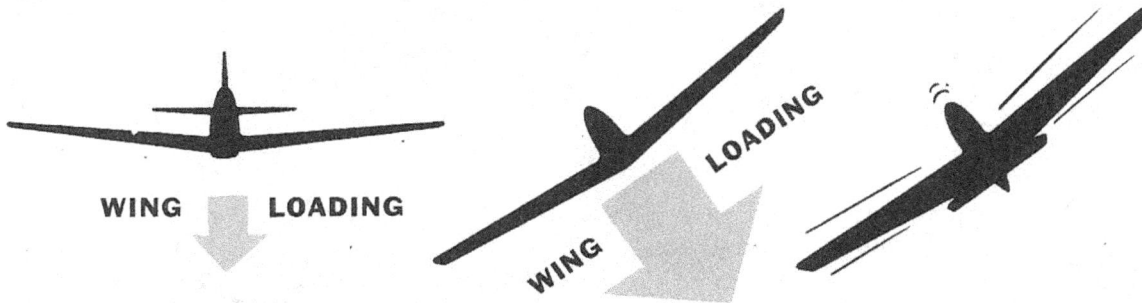

**WING** **LOADING**    **LOADING** **WING**

1. Centrifugal force in a turn increases the wing loading as the angle of bank increases.

2. In order that lift be increased to equal added weight (wing loading) a higher angle of attack is needed. Back pressure on stick.

3. If too much back pressure is applied and the "Critical" angle of attack is reached, the wing will stall, just as in level flight, but good.

## EFFECT OF FLAPS

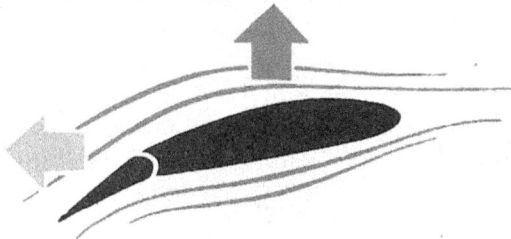

## EFFECT OF AILERONS

Change of camber of wing by use of flaps increases lift and drag components over—

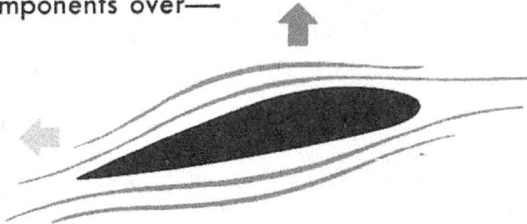

Lowering Aileron at normal speed causes wing to raise.

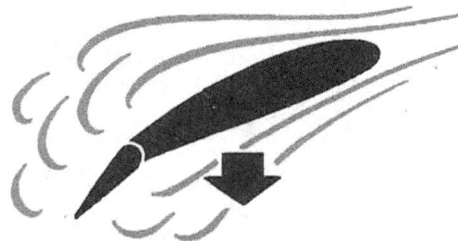

that of wing without flaps, reducing stalling speed. Higher lift permits lower landing speeds. Added drag has an "Airbrake" effect when landing and in landing roll.

Lowering Aileron at near stalling speed increases drag and further aggravates the stalled condition of that wing, causing it to drop. (Raised aileron does not aggravate the stalled condition.)

51

**1** Move the stick forward quickly and smoothly, but **avoid jamming or snapping.**

**2** At the same time advance the throttle in a flowing but rapid movement to the full power position. Move stick and throttle **together!** Don't break the nose too far below the horizon.

**3** Apply opposite rudder at the first indication of a wing dropping.

**4** Immediately after the nose of the airplane is lowered, you will regain minimum flying speed and ailerons will become effec-

tive. Then, if one wing is down, coordinated use of ailerons and rudder will bring about a smoother recovery than rudder alone. **Do not use ailerons too soon.** This causes burbles that aggravate the stall.

**5** Raise the nose to level flight with steady back pressure when you attain safe flying speed (maximum of 95 to 100 mph). AVOID **ABRUPT** CHANGES OF ATTITUDE.

**6** Retard the throttle to cruising rpm **after** leveling off.

### Common Errors of Student

1. Fails to hold the airplane in the required attitude **prior to the stall.**

2. Starts recovery before the stall occurs.

3. Fails to recognize the stall when it occurs.

4. Advances the throttle ahead of the stick or is slow in getting them forward.

5. Snaps the stick forward and goes into a steep dive, losing too much altitude.

6. Uses excessive rudder, producing violent skids.

7. Tries to pick up a wing with ailerons while still stalled.

8. Pulls up nose abruptly, producing secondary stall.

**"THERE IS NO FIXED STALLING SPEED"**

# CHARACTERISTIC STALL

HOLD LANDING ATTITUDE

This brings out the stalling characteristics of the airplane, that is, the approximate stalling speed, tendencies to break to the right or left, etc.

You can learn a lot from this stall. If an airplane breaks sharply to the left, it probably spins faster to the left than to the right; and the left wing will tend to drop if you level off too high when landing. Report any violent characteristics to the engineering office immediately.

Auxiliary Controls: In cruising positions, except throttle fully retarded.

## Procedure

1. Be sure the area is clear, retard the throttle, and hold the airplane in level flight until you reduce flying speed to approximately 90 mph.

2. Lower the nose long enough to establish a normal gliding attitude, flaps up.

3. Raise the nose to landing attitude and hold it there on a point straight ahead until the stall occurs.

4. Allow the airplane to break to the right or left without corrective control. If the break doesn't come at once, keep applying enough back pressure to hold the landing attitude until a break to the right or left **does occur.**

5. When the airplane stalls, note the airspeed, the feel of the airplane and the controls, and the direction and the sharpness of the break.

## Recovery

Postpone recovery until the nose passes through the horizon. Then execute a Standard Stall Recovery, followed by an Approach to a Stall.

53

ABOUT 50°

ESTABLISH AND HOLD
THIS ATTITUDE

IT'S ALL RUDDER

NO AILERON

This demonstrates the proper use of rudder when the airplane is in a stalled condition. It's like riding a bicycle . . . you do all the work with your feet. New students often use too much aileron and **altogether too little** rudder in controlling a stalled airplane.

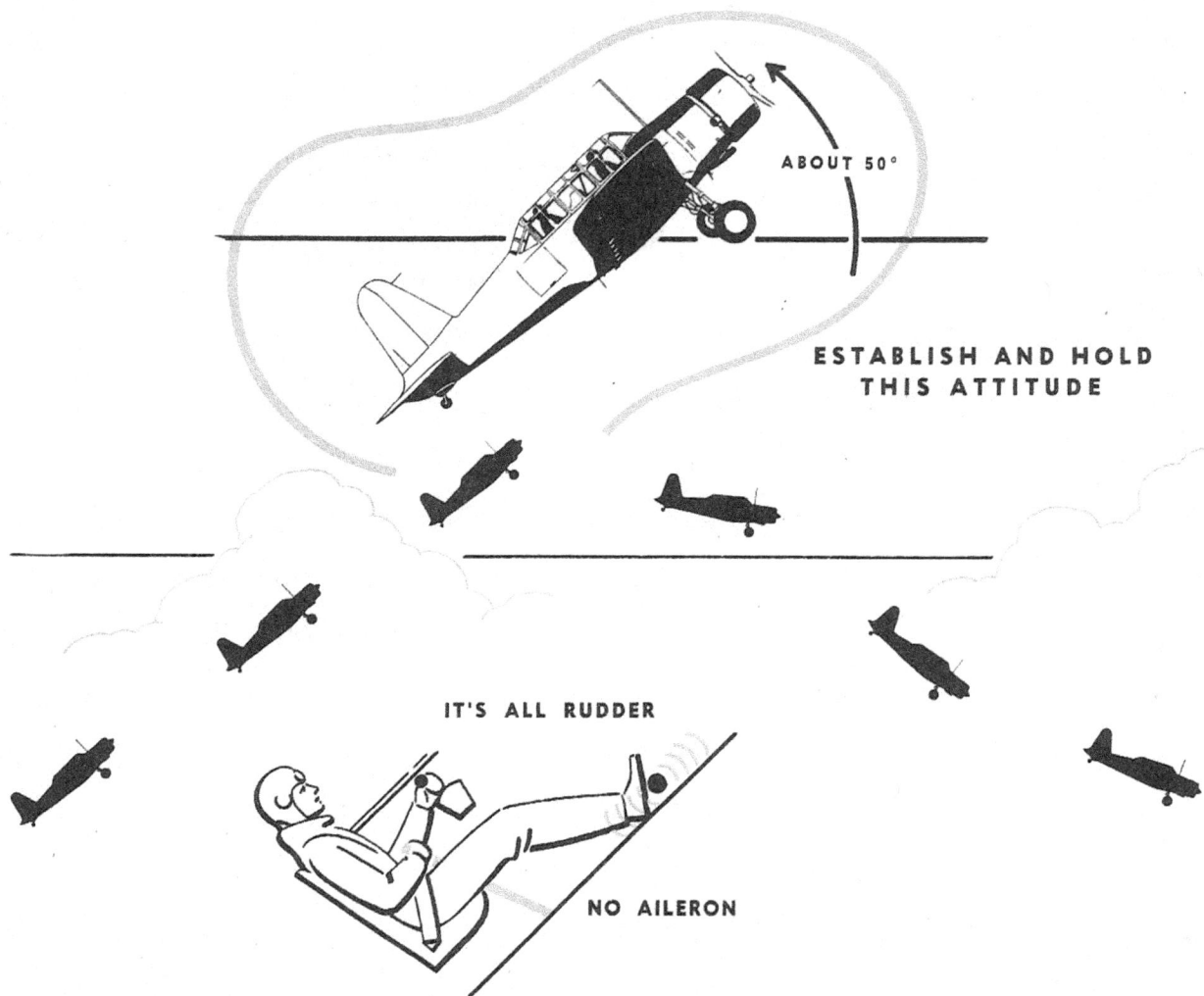

Expert rudder control helps to prevent spins, improves Snap Rolls, Slow Rolls, and other advanced maneuvers, and keeps wings level and the nose straight on a poor landing.

Auxiliary Controls: In cruising positions.

**Procedure**

1. Clear the area, raise the nose to an angle 50° above the horizon and hold it there on a point straight ahead until the stall occurs.

2. As the airplane stalls, bring the stick back smoothly and slowly all the way. **Keep ailerons neutral.**

3. Hold the airplane straight, wings level, with alert movements of the rudder. Think ahead of the airplane and anticipate the need for rudder action. The whole purpose of this stall is to show how much control you can get from the rudder alone.

4. Prolong the stall. Postpone starting recovery until the nose cuts the horizon.

**Recovery**

Execute a Standard Stall Recovery. You may have to drop the nose lower than usual when recovering because of the completely stalled condition.

ABOUT 40°

**ESTABLISH AND HOLD
THIS ATTITUDE**

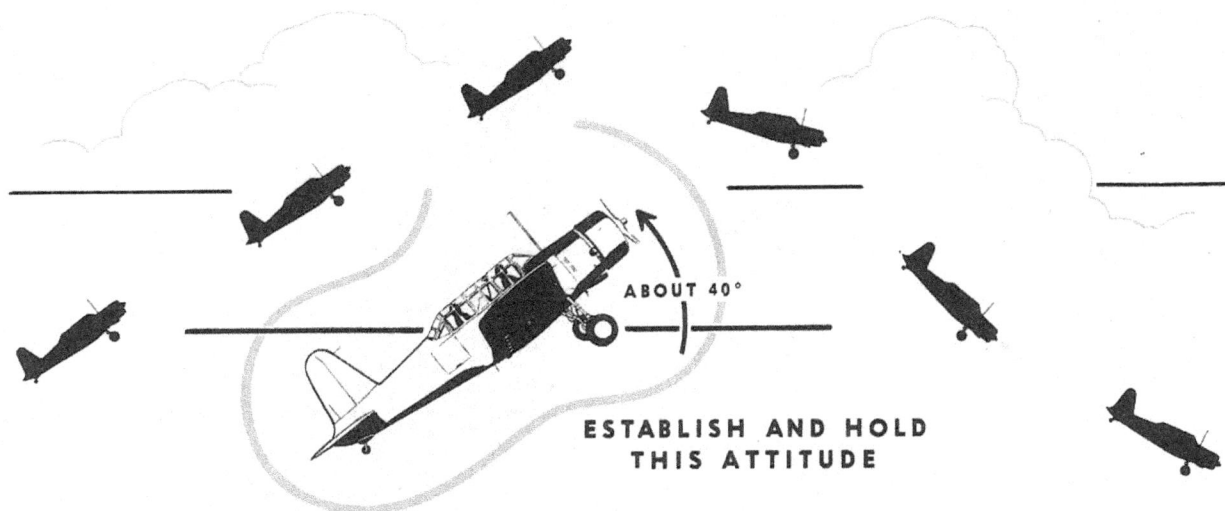

Look! Listen! and Feel! Practice these stalls conscientiously and you'll never unintentionally stall in power-on, climbing attitudes.

Auxiliary Controls: In cruising positions.

### Procedure From Climbs Straight Ahead

1. Be sure the area is clear and raise the nose to an angle 40° above the horizon. Hold that attitude with wings level and nose steady. Correct for torque which increases rapidly as your airspeed decreases.

2. As the stall approaches, note the laxness of controls (especially in back pressure), the laboring of the engine, the strong torque pull, and then the shudder as the airplane stalls.

### Recovery

Normally the airplane will break to the left when it stalls. Apply opposite rudder at the first indication of a wing dropping — and make a Standard Stall Recovery.

### Procedure From Climbing Turns
### To Right or Left

1. Establish a coordinated climbing turn with a bank of approximately 20° and the nose 40° above the horizon. Accomplish this by a blending of rudder, aileron, and back pressure so that you establish bank and turn simultaneously.

2. Hold this attitude and a constant rate of turn by constantly correcting pressures until the stall occurs.

### Recovery

Make a Standard Stall Recovery. Execute a coordinated roll-out as soon as there is sufficient flying speed to make ailerons effective, i.e., use stick and rudder together to bring the airplane back to straight and level flight. Notice the difference in the action of the airplane in right and left stalls. Usually the break to the left will be more pronounced because of the heavy torque pull in that direction.

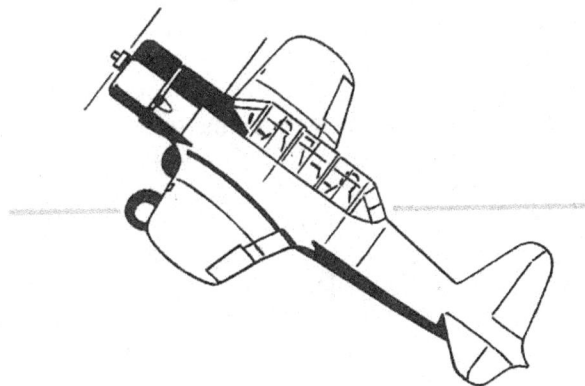

**HOLD THIS ATTITUDE FOR
RIGHT OR LEFT STALL**

**HOLD LANDING ATTITUDE**

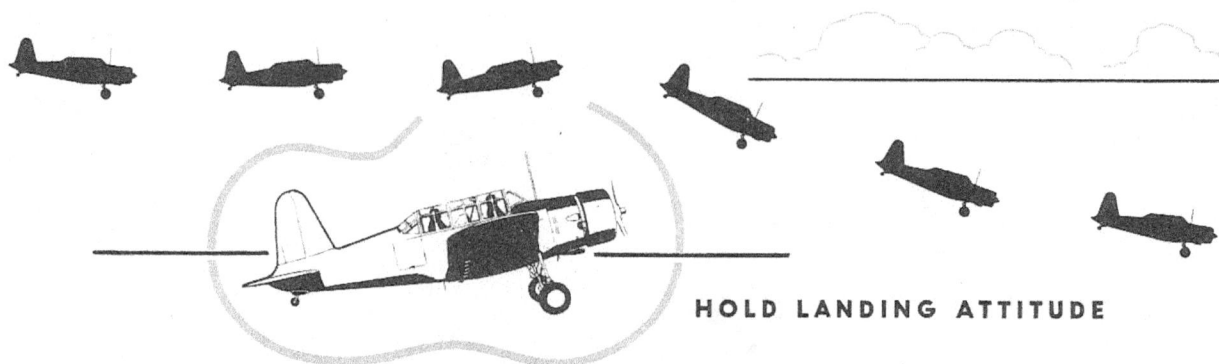

These maneuvers show you how to recognize and how to recover from stalls that sometimes occur during turns in traffic or during landings. The attitudes described are similar to landing and gliding turn attitudes. Thorough knowledge and understanding of these stalls is necessary for safe operation of the airplane.

Auxiliary Controls: In cruising position except throttle retarded.

## Procedure From Glides Straight Ahead

1. Be sure the area is clear, retard the throttle, and hold the airplane in level flight until airspeed is 90 to 95 mph.

2. Lower the nose long enough to establish a normal gliding attitude, flaps up.

3. Raise the nose to landing attitude and hold it there on a point straight ahead until the stall occurs.

4. Use enough left rudder pressure to keep the nose from wandering to the right— a tendency caused by the "rigging" of the airplane which corrects for torque when power is on.

5. As you approach the stall, note the looseness of controls, mushy feeling of the airplane, and rapidly diminishing airspeed. Remember this is like a landing stall.

## Recovery

Execute a Standard Stall Recovery, hesitate in level flight, and retard the throttle to cruising rpm. Then execute an Approach to a Stall straight ahead.

## Procedure From Gliding Turns to the Right or Left

1. Be sure the area is clear, retard the throttle, and hold the airplane in level flight until airspeed is 90 to 95 mph.

2. Establish a normal gliding attitude straight ahead, flaps up.

3. Then roll into a medium gliding turn of 40° of bank. Maintain a steady turn and at the same time slowly raise the nose until it is slightly above the horizon.

4. Hold this position and the angle of bank until a stall occurs. This is a "loss of airspeed" stall and the airplane will usually fall off in the direction of the down wing. This is the type of stall that can occur during turns in traffic.

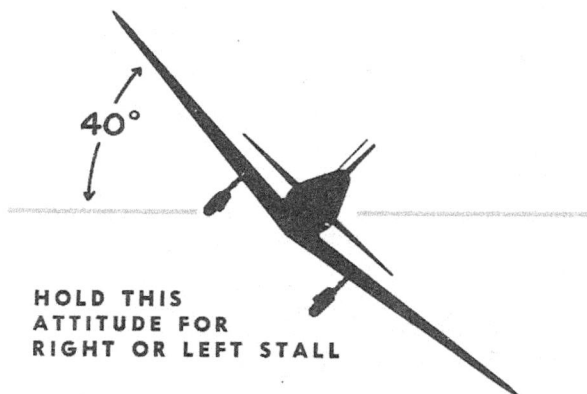

**40°**

**HOLD THIS ATTITUDE FOR RIGHT OR LEFT STALL**

## Recovery

Execute a Standard Stall Recovery, hesitate in level flight, and retard the throttle to approximately cruising rpm. Then execute an Approach to a Stall in the same direction as the gliding turn that led into the stall.

This maneuver shows you how to get maximum performance in climbs without stalling, how to regain lost altitude, and how to feel an approaching stall. It develops your touch and will help you master maximum performance climbing turns and chandelles. Always execute an Approach to a Stall after every power-off stall to regain altitude.

## Procedure After Stalls From a Glide Straight Ahead

1. Establish and hold exactly the same attitude as in a Power-On Normal Recovery Stall straight ahead.

2. When you reach minimum flying speed, lower the nose smoothly to the horizon.

## Procedure After Stalls From a Glide To the Right or Left

1. Blend controls to establish a coordinated climbing turn with a bank of 20° and a 40° angle of climb—exactly the same as the attitude in a normal recovery stall, power on, to the right or left. This attitude is **important!**

2. Maintain this attitude of flight, allowing airspeed to dissipate.

3. Time your roll-out so that the wings are back level again (nose still high) just as you reach minimum flying speed.

4. Hesitate long enough to check your attitude and then lower the nose to the horizon to avoid stalling.

STRAIGHT AHEAD
HOLD THIS ATTITUDE

ABOUT 40°

HESITATE, THEN LOWER
NOSE TO HORIZON

ROLL LEVEL AND MAINTAIN
ANGLE OF CLIMB

HOLD THIS
ATTITUDE

ESTABLISH POWER ON
NORMAL RECOVERY
STALL ATTITUDE

APPROACH TO A STALL
TO RIGHT OR LEFT

AFTER STALL RECOVERY
THROTTLE TO CRUISING

# DEMONSTRATION STALLS

Too much stick, too much rudder, or incorrect trimming may force the airplane into unusual stall positions. Demonstration Stalls give you a clear picture of these positions and show you how to recover from each.

## Keep Your Head

Don't let these stalls frighten you. Your instructor has practiced all these stalls dozens of times, and knows what he is doing. Certain Demonstration Stalls may put the airplane into a spin or cause it to execute a snap roll. Don't let this startle you. Keep alert to what is happening.

When the instructor lets you practice Demonstration Stalls, notice **how much** pressure it takes to stall the airplane and how easy it is to recover when you know how. Remember that stalls like these don't occur unless you **make them happen** by improper use of controls or inexpert flying. These stalls teach you what **not to do!**

---

**RECOVERY STARTED**

## Procedure

1. Execute a Normal Recovery Stall — Power On, straight ahead. During recovery raise the nose rapidly before you regain adequate flying speed, so that a Secondary Stall occurs before the nose reaches the horizon.

2. Secondary Stalls are usually more violent than the original one, losing more airspeed and more altitude. Such stalls can be disastrous when they occur close to the ground. Always practice stalls at a safe altitude, minimum of 4,000 ft.

## Recovery

Execute a Standard Stall Recovery.

**PULL-OUT TOO ABRUPT**

## SECONDARY STALLS

When you pull the nose up too abruptly during the recovery from a stall the airplane will stagger into a Secondary Stall. It will vibrate, rattle, and call you names.

*OK*

# STABILIZER STALL

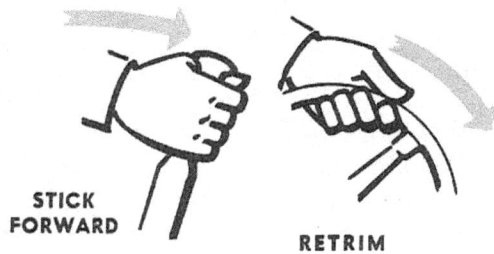

STICK FORWARD

RETRIM

TO RECOVER

TRIM FOR GLIDE

OPEN THROTTLE

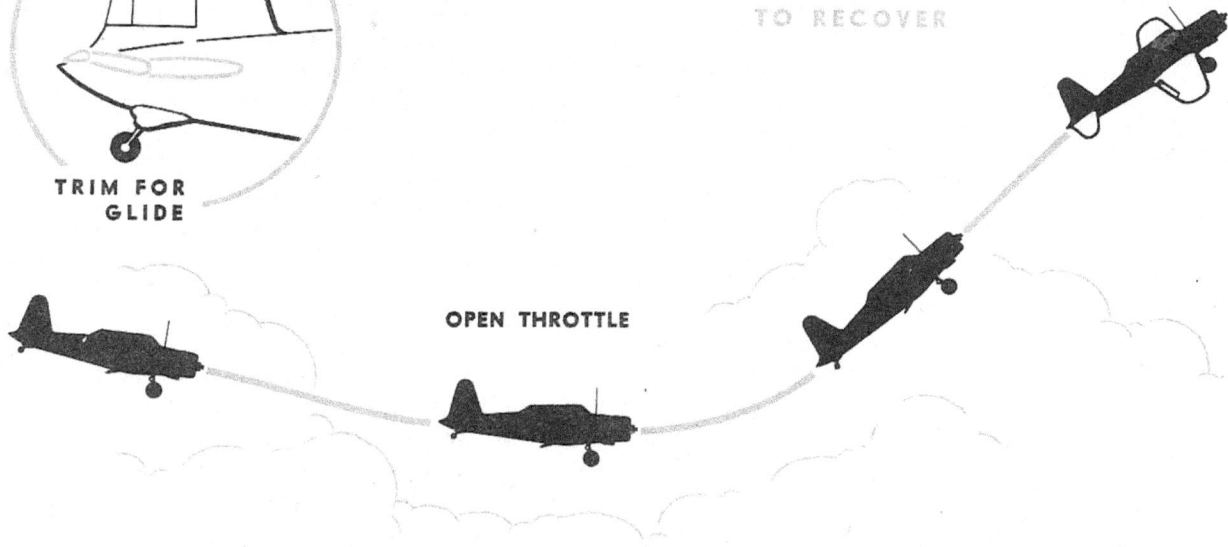

This dramatizes what can happen, after a bad approach for a landing or after a simulated forced landing, if you slam on the throttle without holding the nose down and without adjusting the elevator trim tab. Stabilizer Stalls happen fast and are dangerous if they occur close to the ground.

Auxiliary Controls: In landing positions on Vultee Trainer.

## Procedure

1. Be sure the area is clear, retard throttle, change to high rpm, roll down 20° of flaps, and establish a normal glide straight ahead.

2. Trim the elevator so that you can maintain your glide with **no back pressure at all.**

3. Relax on the controls and give it full throttle. The airplane will zoom up and stall and it may snap on its back and spin if not righted promptly.

## Recovery

Force the nose down with strong forward stick and adjust the elevator trim tab quickly.

Be especially alert on recovery. Too violent a stall may throw the airplane into some position that will build up too much airspeed for the flaps.

Use the best recovery for the position and action of the airplane. If it reaches an inverted position, decide quickly whether to stop the snap with forward stick and opposite rudder or to complete the snap roll.

DO NOT EXCEED 120 MPH

IN THE BASIC AIRPLANE

WITH FLAPS DOWN

# EXCESSIVE BACK-STICK STALLS
## (Power On)

These stalls show that an airplane can be stalled at normal cruising speed by simply using **too much** back pressure. Practicing this stall will show you how much is too much.

Auxiliary Controls: In cruising position.

### Procedure From Steep Turns
### To the Right or Left

1. Be sure the area is clear and then roll the airplane into a steep turn (60° to 70° angle of bank).
2. Rapidly build up back pressure on the stick.

3. The airplane will immediately stall. Note the airspeed, the bucking and buffeting of the airplane, and how much back pressure it takes to force the airplane into this stall.

### Recovery

You can usually recover quickly by relieving the back pressure on the stick. In a more violent stall it may be necessary to execute a Standard Stall Recovery.

Stalls caused by too much pressure on controls, rather than by loss of airspeed, are often referred to as Accelerated Stalls.

# EXCESSIVE TOP AND BOTTOM RUDDER STALLS
## (Power On)

What happens when you use too much rudder during maximum performance power-on maneuvers? The airplane will probably perform a snap roll or enter a spin immediately. The stalls described here demonstrate how **not** to use the rudder and the correct recovery from excessive rudder stalls.

Auxiliary Controls: In cruising position.

### Procedure From Steep Turns
### To the Right and Left

1. Be sure the area is clear and then roll the airplane into a steep turn (60° to 70° of bank).
2. Hold back stick pressure **normal** for steep turns.
3. Build up excessive top or bottom rudder pressure rapidly. The airplane will nor-

mally snap in the direction of the rudder used; to the left, for example, in a steep left turn if you use bottom rudder, and to the right if you use top rudder.

### Recovery

In less sharp breaks, opposite rudder will stop the snap or spin; but if the airplane starts a **strong** snap roll, for example, it may be better to complete the roll. If you attempt to roll back against the built-up momentum of the snap, you may stop on your back, delaying recovery and losing time and altitude.

Such stalls don't occur unless the controls are manhandled, and they are no hazard to an alert pilot. If you make the most of stall practice, you'll quickly learn how much control pressure you can use without stalling.

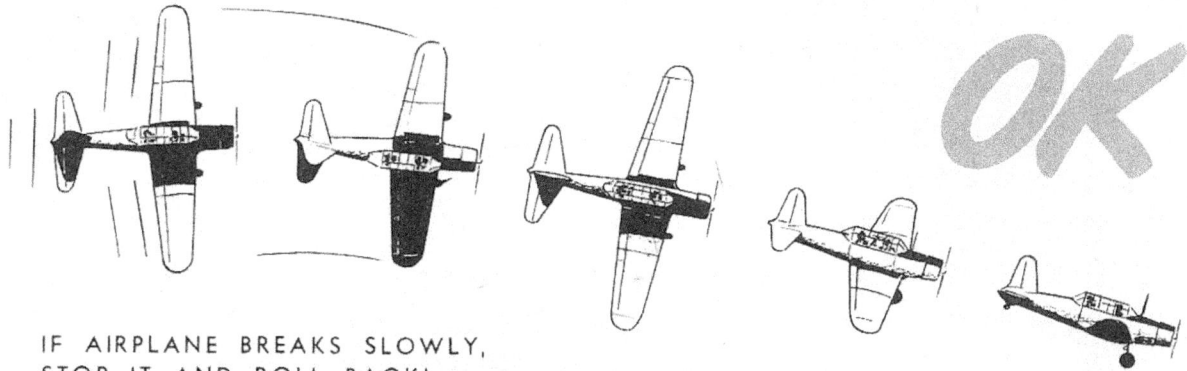

IF AIRPLANE BREAKS SLOWLY,
STOP IT AND ROLL BACK!

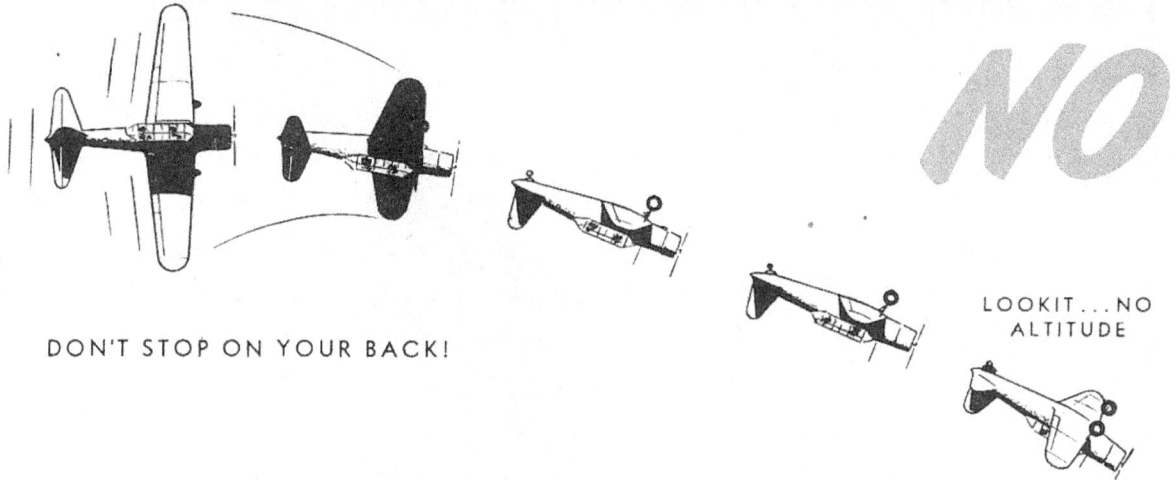

OK

DON'T STOP ON YOUR BACK!

NO

LOOKIT...NO
ALTITUDE

IF AIRPLANE BREAKS SHARPLY,
FOLLOW ROLL THROUGH!

OK

Sometimes, when making turns in traffic, students add more and more rudder pressure to increase the rate of turn and build up opposite aileron to keep the bank from getting too steep. This can produce a Cross-Control Stall which occurs suddenly, almost without warning. Cross-Control Stalls teach you how to avoid this **dangerous** error.

Auxiliary Controls: In cruising position.

## Procedure

1. Be sure the area is clear, retard the throttle, and hold the airplane in level flight until airspeed is 90 to 95 mph.

2. Establish a normal gliding turn to the left or right.

3. Keep building up rudder pressure to increase the rate of turn and keep adding opposite aileron to maintain a normal bank.

4. Note the pronounced skid which will result and note that the airplane breaks with **practically no warning**. It just goes "whoosh!" Usually it will dip suddenly into a spin or execute a snap roll, out of control.

5. Close to the ground this is one of the **most dangerous things** that can happen. A persistent tendency to cross controls in gliding turns will **not be tolerated**.

## Recovery

You can recover quickly and easily if you start in time — forward stick and opposite rudder will stop the stall. But if the airplane gets a good start into a snap roll or a spin, you may have to complete the roll or use a spin recovery.

DANGER: Controls Crossed!

*Spins*

# POWER OFF AND POWER ON

The Basic Trainer is a good airplane in which to practice spins because it has normal spin characteristics and at the same time spins steeply and rapidly enough to adequately demonstrate this maneuver.

Any average student can quickly learn spin recoveries because they are done by formula instead of by feel. You will use the tested and approved *NACA spin recovery developed by the world's best test pilots. Most difficulties in learning spins can be traced directly to a student's own nervousness. Lay your doubts aside, learn the proper entry and recovery point by point, and you'll find that a spin is one of the easiest maneuvers of all.

## What Happens in a Spin?

It helps to know what happens in a spin. The airplane is in a stalled condition. It starts to rotate about its center of gravity with the inside wing down slightly and completely stalled. The outside wing is higher, is moving faster and at a lower angle of attack. It is somewhat less stalled and retains a certain amount of lift. This unequal stalled condition of the wings tends to rotate the airplane. Once a spin is started the airplane tends to keep spinning as long as controls are held with the spin. This is called auto-rotation.

The result is that the airplane will not respond to the usual control pressures. The use of ailerons merely stirs up burbles about the wings and aggravates the stalled condition.

A special control technique, simple but different, is necessary. A spin recovery is the one maneuver in flying that is almost entirely mechanical . . . like executing "Left Shoulder —Arms!" You learn a given sequence of movements and that's it.

## How Spins Affect the Pilot

It is perfectly normal for too many turns to cause a certain amount of vertigo or dizziness in a healthy pilot. Only deaf mutes and the insane can be whirled about without experiencing dizziness.

Spins of one to three turns won't noticeably affect the vast majority of pilots. However, it is inadvisable to spin more than three turns because each additional turn increases the degree of dizziness.

The pilot who does become dizzy during a spin may have a strong sensation as he recovers that the airplane is spinning in the opposite direction. Instinctively he may try to execute a recovery from this imaginary spin and thus put the airplane into a secondary spin in the same direction as the original one.

The important things to remember are:

1. Don't try spins of more than three turns. You may get dizzy.

2. If you are dizzy as the airplane recovers from a spin, don't let your sensations fool you. Don't try to recover from an imaginary spin.

## Spin Schedule

You will have a chance to practice both Power-On and Power-Off spins during the first week of flying and will practice spins during every dual transition flight throughout the course. Your instructor will demonstrate three-turn spins before you solo. Remember that you are not to practice solo spins until they are scheduled.

Keep your mind clear and your eyes and ears open. Your instructor won't solo you until he is confident that you can satisfactorily perform spin recoveries. Stay relaxed and take your time. Memorize the proper entry and recovery and you'll know exactly what to do and when to do it.

*National Advisory Committee on Aeronautics.

### Altitudes

Enter spins at or above the following altitudes:

One-turn or two-turn spins — 5,000 ft. above the ground. Spins of more than two turns — 7,000 ft. above the ground. Three-turn spins are the maximum authorized in Basic Training.

Auxiliary Controls: In cruising position.

# HOW TO ENTER SPINS

### Power-Off Entry

**1** Clear the area with special care and fully retard the throttle.

**2** Raise the nose 20° to 30° above the horizon. It is a common error to raise the nose too high, producing an irregular spin with the nose dipping up and down.

**3** As the airplane approaches the stall, feed in rudder in the direction of the spin.

**4** As the stall occurs, use full hard rudder **all the way** in the direction of the spin and bring the stick **straight back all the way** and hold it there. You will immediately enter the spin.

### Power-On Entry

Entry is identical with Power-Off Spins except:

1. At cruising throttle raise the nose 30° to 40° above the horizon.

2. Cut the throttle all the way when the nose slices through the horizon into the spin.

### IMPORTANT:

Hold controls all the way in these extreme positions to produce a steady spin and to make controls more effective on recovery. If controls are relaxed, you will usually spiral and gain too much diving speed.

### Secondary Spins and Emergency Spins

Remember that a spin is just another maneuver. There is no need to get rushed and excited or to lose your head. Keep calm, keep cool, take your time. You can't rush a spin recovery. Snapping the stick back too fast when recovering from the dive may cause a secondary stall and possibly a spin.

Another common error is to fail to neutralize the rudder when the spinning stops so that you snap into a spin in the opposite direction. Combinations of these errors can result in sudden and violent secondary spins.

Spins are never dangerous if the pilot maintains self-control and recovers the way he has been taught. When you are executing a recovery, don't start a new one until you have made **at least three turns** with controls full against the spin. Many an airplane has been unnecessarily abandoned in a moment of excitement because the pilot lost his head or was frightened when the airplane didn't recover immediately. This occasionally occurs because it takes time for the new position of controls to become effective. Normally the airplane will stop spinning if controls are held against the spin **long enough.**

It is practically never necessary to abandon the Basic airplane in spins unless the airfoils have been altered or damaged, or the center of gravity abnormally changed.

When to bail out is a problem of altitude. If you have used the proper recovery techniques, have held the controls for three to five turns against the spin without success, and if you are running out of altitude, then don't wait. Get out! If you decide to bail out, leave the airplane quickly at 1,000 ft. above the ground or higher (see parachute section).

### Common Errors of Student

1. Fails to clear the area.

2. Starts the spin at too low an altitude.

3. Makes faulty entry into the spin.

4. Does not hold the controls all the way with the spin. Fails to keep ailerons in neutral.

5. Is unable to orient himself in a spin.

6. Doesn't wait long enough between opposite rudder and forward stick.

7. Doesn't hold controls all the way against the spin long enough.

8. Fails to neutralize controls properly at the right time.

9. Dives airplane excessively in recovery.

**1** Be sure throttle is completely retarded, stick is all the way back and rudder is full with the spin.

**2** Briskly apply FULL opposite rudder.

**3** After applying opposite rudder, keep the stick ALL THE WAY BACK until you complete one-quarter to one-half turn; then BRISKLY move the stick ALL THE WAY forward.

**4** Hold controls in these extreme positions AGAINST THE SPIN UNTIL the spinning stops. Then neutralize rudder and recover from the resulting dive.

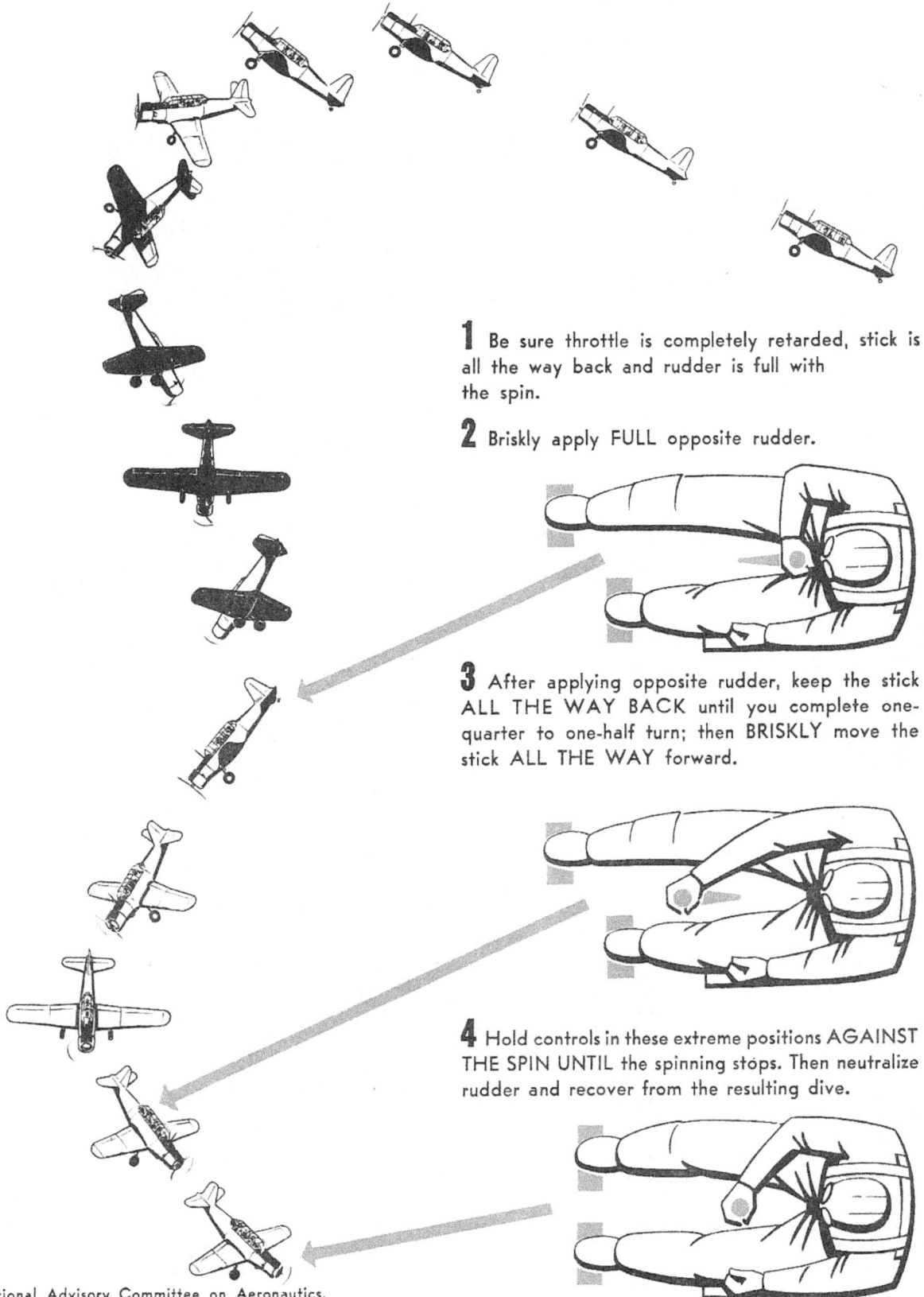

*National Advisory Committee on Aeronautics.

# SIMULATED FORCED LANDINGS

PICK A FIELD—
WHAT FIELD?
GLIDE—TURN—
YES—NO—
DOWNWIND
UPWIND
YES—
OH—
OH—

You are flying along and suddenly your engine quits. What to do? You have to act quickly. Where's the best place to set down with the least damage to yourself and the airplane? Of all the maneuvers in flying training, the Simulated Forced Landing is probably the most fun and at the same time highly practical. It develops lightning reactions and sharpens your judgment of speed, distance, and satisfactory places to land.

Forced Landing practice is a highly important part of Basic Training. It is started during the first week of the course and, after that, you can expect one or several Forced Landings during every dual transition ride throughout the course.

### Proficiency

Don't get discouraged if you don't come in perfectly at first. There is a lot to do in a brief time and it takes practice. What your instructor is most interested in is your progress. At first he'll be watching what you do in the cockpit, your turns and your glides, and won't worry much about whether you hit the field or not. Within a few weeks he'll expect good judgment in selecting a field, a logical approach pattern, and a smooth gliding technique. Later he will demand proficiency in all phases of Forced Landings.

### "Forced Landing!"

Most instructors use three methods of giving Forced Landings. The instructor may simply shout, "Forced Landing!" and leave you on your own to see what you'll do; or he may ask you to point out the field you have selected. Sometimes, at a higher altitude, he may point out the field you are to use.

Expect a Forced Landing whenever you are flying at 1,000 ft. above the ground or lower. It is a favorite move among instructors to call one when you are doing 8's Along a Road or flying to or from your practice area.

Remember, **you** are flying the airplane and **you** are handling stick and rudder. The instructor is handling the throttle. Don't fly too close to the ground, and always watch out for obstructions ahead.

After each period in the air, sit down and review your Forced Landings. Analyze your errors. Your instructor will bite his nails down to his elbows if you keep making the same mistakes over and over.

### How to Select a Field

1. First look ahead and to the sides and then, if high enough, bank to look below and behind.

2. Consider the wind direction and velocity. **Always** know these or your instructor will have a nervous breakdown.

3. You can probably get into any field that is inside of an angle sighted at 45° from the airplane to the ground. This is a rough guide only and will vary with wind direction and velocity.

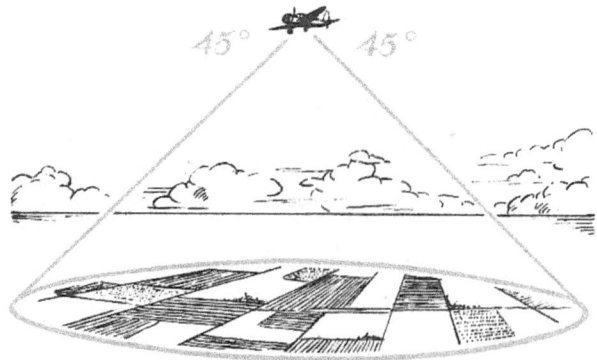

4. Pick a field that is long enough for a safe landing; remember that the wider the field is, the better opportunity you have on the base leg to correct for errors in judgment of time and distance.

5. Choose pastures or cleared open fields if they are free of ditches, fences, boulders, livestock, and other obstructions. Cultivated fields are satisfactory if the crops are not too high. Plowed fields are unsafe after a rain, and grown corn is dangerous.

If possible, plan to land **with** the furrows and **against** the wind. If there is a strong wind at 90° to the furrows, it **may** be better to land **across** the furrows.

## Planning the Approach

The secret of a successful Forced Landing is in planning the approach so the airplane will arrive at the key point on the base leg at traffic altitude. From there on, it's simply another landing.

Avoid long, straight approaches from high altitudes and approaches in which the field is concealed during the glide. Use simple, logical approaches to a normal base leg.

## Glides and Turns

Hold airspeed 5 to 10 miles an hour above a normal glide, establish a normal glide on the base leg, and shoot for a point half way up the field to avoid undershooting. Overshooting usually can be controlled by flaps.

Strive for precision in gliding turns and make the last turn into the field at about 500 ft. (never below 300 feet). Never "S" or turn on the final approach and don't get excited—it only creates confusion.

## Common Errors of Student

1. Lands downwind or crosswind.
2. Lets airspeed get dangerously low.
3. Makes a poor selection of fields.
4. Changes mind at last minute. (Pick a pattern and field and stay with them.)
5. Fails to establish a proper glide. (A poor glide will spoil the maneuver.)
6. Makes dangerously low turns.

**Note:** As in any landing, difficulty near the ground can usually be traced to improper maneuvering higher up. Analyze your errors with this in mind.

# STANDARD PROCEDURE FOR FORCED LANDINGS

HERE IS A PLAY-BY-PLAY DESCRIPTION OF A GOOD FORCED LANDING PROCEDURE IN THE BT-13A:

**1** Instructor cuts the throttle, announces, "Forced Landing!"

**2** Student shouts, "Gas!", checks the fuel supply, changes tanks only if necessary, moves the propeller control forward to High rpm, and rolls down 20° of flaps (on Vultee Trainer).

**3** Student establishes a normal glide, rolls elevator trim back, and opens or indicates the canopy, meanwhile looking for a suitable landing field.

**4** Student plans his approach to bring the airplane to traffic altitude on the base leg as in a regular landing.

**5** After the last turn on the final approach, student shouts, "Flaps" at the moment he would lower them, but DOES NOT actually lower additional flaps.

**6** At 250 feet above the ground (never lower), you can judge the landing and the INSTRUCTOR opens the throttle.

**7** Student holds the nose down while adjusting elevator trim and flies the airplane away.

*No Solo Simulated Forced Landings*

67

# Radio

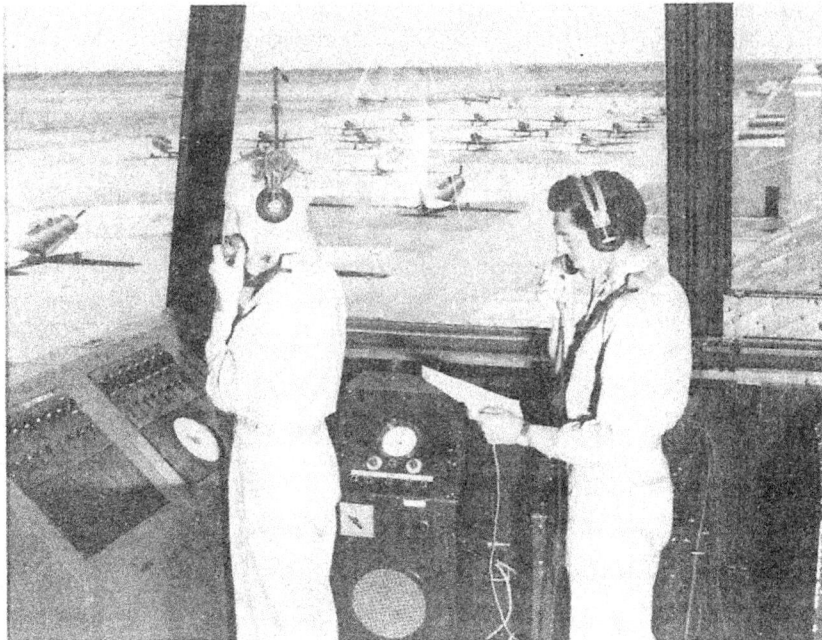

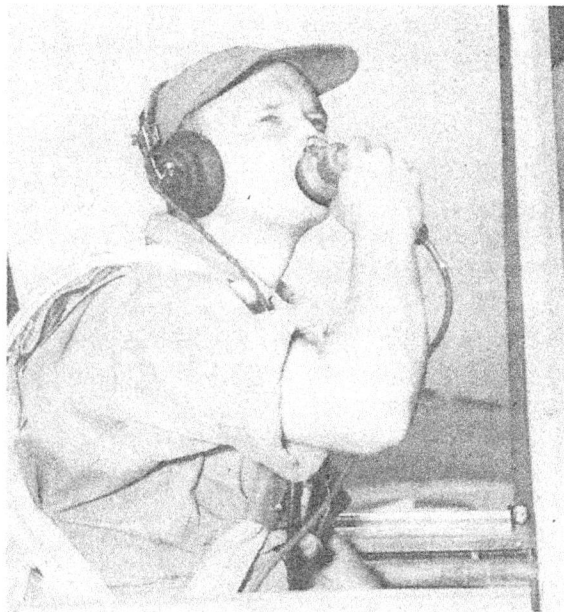

Airplane radio is brand new to you. It is a mysterious device until you become acquainted with it—then it is relatively simple. The only way you will learn all about your radio is to dig in and study it. Read about it. Ask the engineer about it. Study the Pilots' Information File. Some day your knowledge may save your neck because you can do a lot of tricks with radio if you know how.

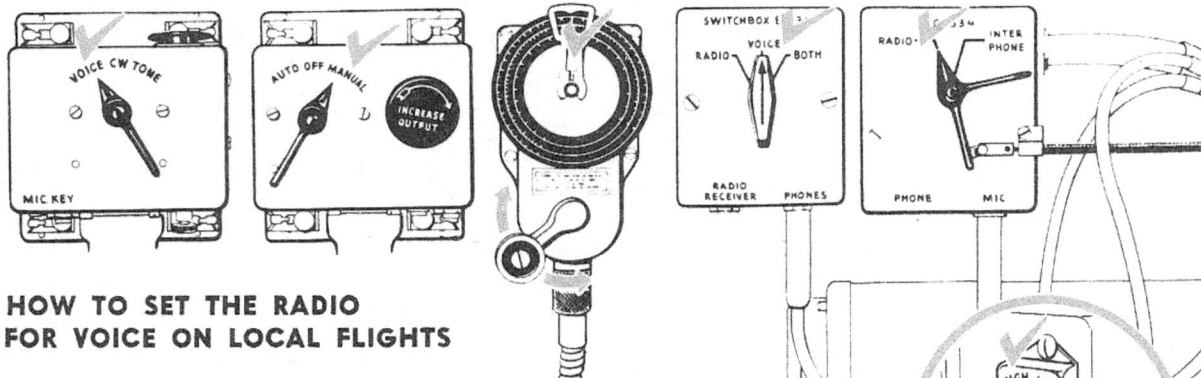

## HOW TO SET THE RADIO
## FOR VOICE ON LOCAL FLIGHTS

1. Ignition Switch ON, or radio won't work.

2. Transmitter Switch (Voice, CW, Tone) on VOICE.

3. Receiver Control (Auto, Off, Manual) on MANUAL.

4. Volume Control LOUD. Radio fades during take-off and as you get farther from the field.

5. Filter Switch (Voice, Range, Both) on VOICE.

6. Radio-Interphone Switch on RADIO.

7. Hi-Lo switch on HI to receive the training frequency.

### How to Tune the Radio

1. Turn the tuning dial a little to each side of the frequency mark to find the point where the signal is strongest.

2. Use the **outer** scale on the tuning dial for Hi Coil reception. (Hi-Lo switch on HI.)

### If the Radio Won't Work

1. Check all connections. Are your earphones plugged in?

2. Is the Hi-Lo switch "clicked" on HI?

3. Move the volume control back and forth to test for short circuit. Should work best on LOUD.

4. Check the filter switch on VOICE. You won't get "Voice" if it's on "Range."

5. Is the transmitter switch between positions?

6. Are you tuned to the right frequency?

7. Push the microphone button **down** to transmit.

8. Remember that most radio failures are caused by improper operation. In an emergency, don't give up. Keep trying, check all settings, keep calling, and keep listening.

### How to Use the Radio

**CAUTION:** Don't be handling your microphone when you need both hands to fly the airplane—while taxiing, landing, taking off, etc.

1. Always check your radio before take-off to be sure it is working and is set and tuned properly.

2. Tune carefully before you start to talk so you'll be able to hear the response.

3. Think what you are going to say before you speak. Don't "hem" and "haw."

4. **Listen,** before you squeeze the microphone button so you won't interrupt another transmission.

5. Use approved radio conversation. (See Pilots' Information File.)

6. Hold the microphone properly and speak squarely into it. If you hold it sidewise, you'll transmit engine noise.

7. Squeeze the microphone button to transmit, and release it when you finish talking.

8. Don't shout. Speak slowly and distinctly and **be brief.**

9. Never transmit vulgar or profane language.

10. Give your call letters to identify yourself before each transmission. "Randolph Tower this is P Four Two—."

11. End every transmission with:

    a. "Over"... if a response is expected.

    b. "Out"... if no response is expected.

12. Use "Roger" to mean "I received your last message." Use "Wilco" to mean "I received your message and will comply with it."

13. Tune and use your radio on every flight. You don't have to talk to learn how to use it. Keep your earphones on . . . there may be an emergency message for you. Limit your conversations to those authorized at your field except in emergencies.

14. Never hang your earphones near the instrument panel. Instruments will be magnetized and will not function properly.

15. Be sure your headset fits and is in good working order if you want to hear clearly.

### Information on Radio

Here is more detailed information on your radio. Dig into this. Ask questions about anything that isn't clear. Find out why certain frequencies are used for certain purposes. You'll be glad you know radio when you find yourself flying a fighter airplane across to Africa.

### The Command Set

Most Basic Trainers are equipped with a type SCR-283 Command set consisting of Receiver Unit, Transmitter Unit, and an Interphone System.

### Transmitter Control Unit

The transmitter operates on the training frequency between 2,500 and 7,700 kilocycles at which the radio technician has set it. The coil may be changed to vary this frequency. The transmitter will send Voice, Modulated CW (MCW), or straight CW signals.

**VOICE:** Use this to **talk.** It is the weakest type of transmission, with a range of 10 to 25 miles depending on terrain, atmosphere, etc.

**CW (Continuous Wave):** This is used for telegraphy (key) transmission, and has the longest range. If you get a steady tone when the microphone button is down, you are probably on CW instead of "Voice." The disadvantage of straight CW is that a receiving station (such as a range station) "standing by" a particular frequency, expecting voice signals, will not receive CW unless the receiver is equipped with a beat frequency oscillator that is turned on.

**TONE:** Modified carrier wave, longer range than "Voice," shorter range than CW. Used for telegraphy (key) transmission. Can be picked up by standard receiver equipment that is guarding the transmitting frequency and expecting "Voice."

### Choice of Transmission

Students should **always** use "Voice" except in extreme emergencies when they can try "Tone" telegraphy. Use radio range identification letters to obtain a reply on the range frequency (see Radio Facility Chart). Once a pilot makes contact with "Tone," he can usually continue by "Voice." Tone telegraphy will be heard where CW may not. Although it is often difficult to make contact with CW, it reaches farther after contact is made.

### Receiver Control Unit

The Receiver Control Switch is the master switch and has three positions:

**OFF:** Radio is turned off.

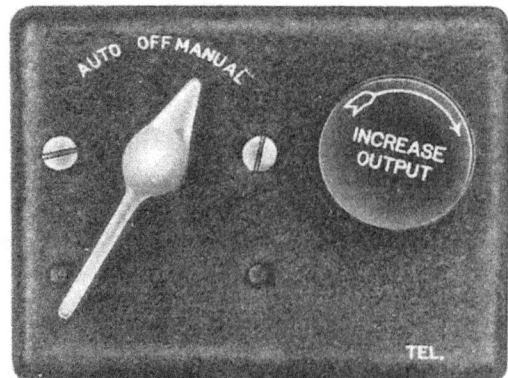

**AUTO:** Acts as an automatic volume control. To use it, tune the receiver first on "Manual," adjust the volume, switch to "Auto" and readjust volume. Volume will then automatically stay at that level as the pilot flies toward or away from the field. Don't use "Auto" for beam flying because the "build-up" and "fade-out" of signal is destroyed. "Auto" is seldom used in Basic Training.

**MANUAL:** This is the most commonly used setting and acts as a fixed volume control. Reception will vary in volume with changes in distance from the field. Use for beam flying.

### Volume Control

Control volume with this knob. Tune **Loud** before take-off because of quick fade during and after take-off.

### Tuning Unit

This is the frequency selector for the receiver. It functions much like any radio Tuning dial but has three scales:

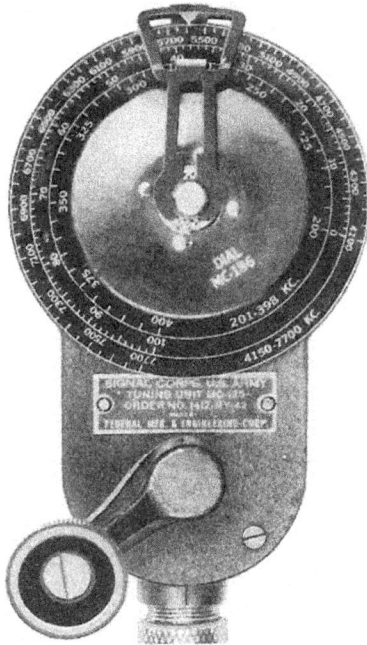

**OUTSIDE SCALE** is graduated from 4,100 to 7,700 kilocycles and includes most training frequencies. To receive these frequencies, put Hi-Lo switch on "HI" and turn to the particular frequency. The coil in the receiver will receive a given range of frequencies such

as 5,500 to 7,700. Frequencies from 4,100 to 5,500 would require a change of coils.

**CENTER SCALE** is graduated from 0 to 100, numbers which **do not** represent kilocycles. This scale can be disregarded unless the special frequencies which require it are being used at your field.

**INSIDE SCALE** is graduated from 200 to 400 kilocycles. Control towers and radio range stations transmit on these frequencies. (See Radio Facility Chart.) To tune in, put the Hi-Lo switch on LO and turn the dial to the desired frequency on this scale.

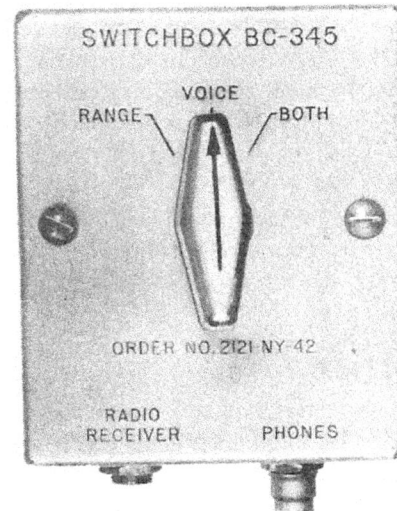

### Filter Unit

This switch box lets the pilot select "Voice" or "Range" reception with minimum interference. It has three settings:

**VOICE:** Filters out "Range" signals and lets "Voice" come through clearly.

**RANGE:** Filters out "Voice" and lets "Range" signals come through clearly.

**BOTH:** Allows both "Voice" and "Range" signals to come through. Use "Both" for maximum volume.

# Coordination Exercise

Maximum Performance flying requires proper coordination of controls which comes only with practice. The Basic airplane is new to you and you may have to change many habits formed in Primary. Coordination Exercises teach you the feel of your new airplane.

Good coordination does not stop simply with moving stick and rudder together. It requires constant changing of pressures to establish or to maintain a given attitude of flight. The student who develops a "fine" touch in the Basic airplane can apply the same general principles to tactical aircraft. Do coordination exercises at every opportunity. Don't waste time in the air because you are simply wasting your own chances of becoming a better pilot. Make every minute count.

Auxiliary Controls: In cruising positions.

## Procedure

1. Pick two points on the horizon separated by an angle of approximately 45° to 60°.

2. Roll into a medium bank that will carry the nose along the horizon to one point and then roll back into an equivalent bank in the opposite direction. The object is to move the nose back and forth from one point to another in a smooth, flowing action, executing uniform degrees of bank in each direction while holding a constant altitude and a constant rate of turn.

3. Start using a medium bank and then steepen it as you become proficient.

## Common Errors of Student

1. Fails to maintain constant altitude.

2. Makes bank steeper in one direction than another.

3. Movements are jerky. Lack smoothness.

4. Stays in bank too long before rolling in the opposite direction.

5. Fails to apply rudder and aileron together, or uses too much rudder with too little aileron, or vice versa.

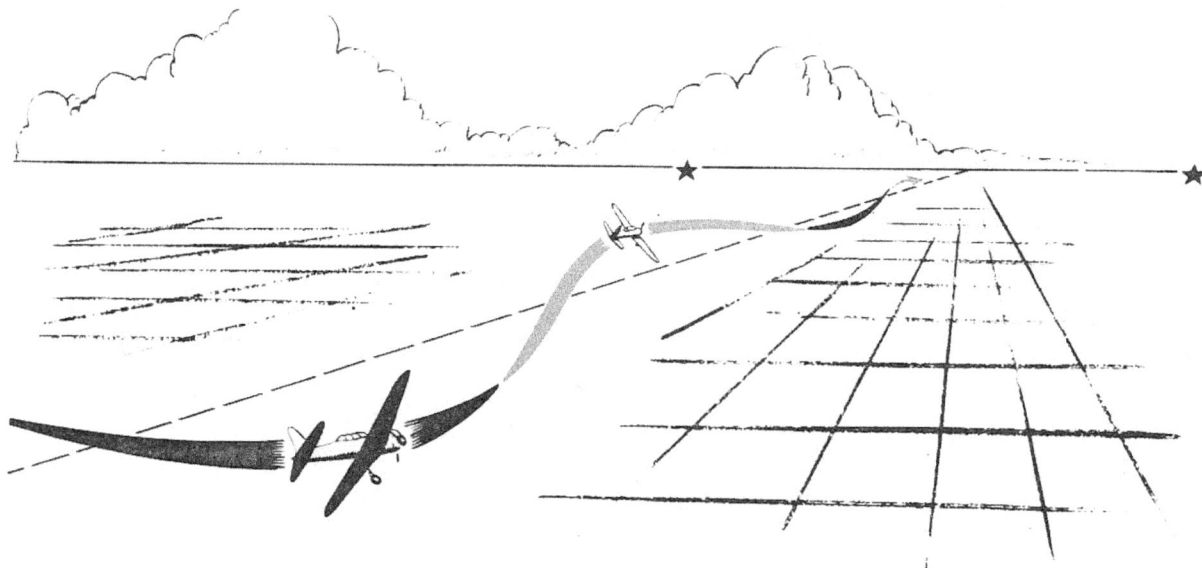

# EIGHTS ALONG A ROAD

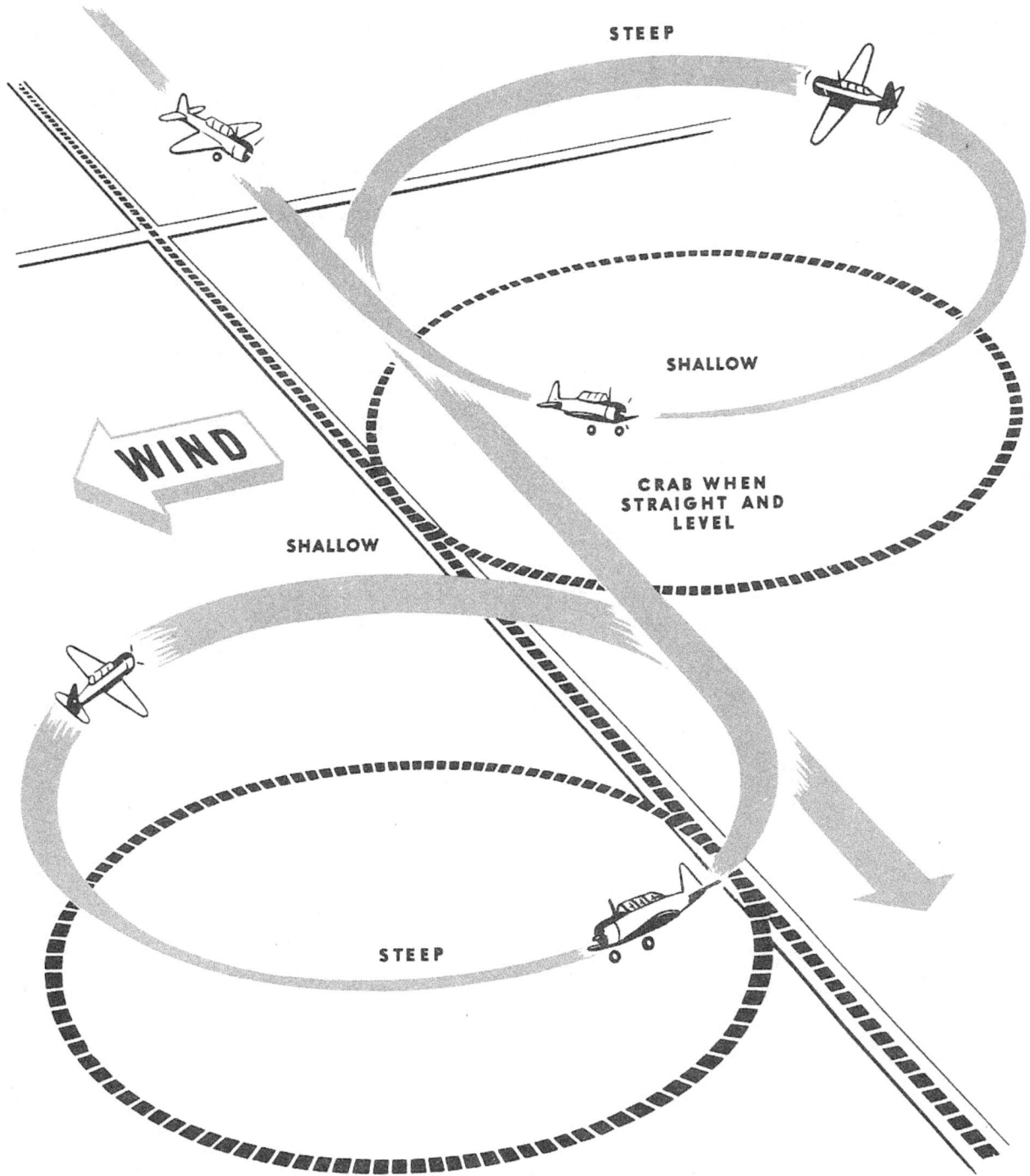

STEEP

SHALLOW

CRAB WHEN
STRAIGHT AND
LEVEL

WIND

SHALLOW

STEEP

This is a simple maneuver to understand, but difficult to perform perfectly. It requires good control, judgment, and planning. Eights Along a Road give you excellent practice in judging and correcting for drift. They also teach you how to fly when watching outside objects, how to plan ahead, how to fly close to the ground, how to judge traffic altitude, and how much space is necessary for a 360° turn.

Auxiliary Controls: In cruising positions.

### Procedure

1. Select a road as nearly perpendicular to the wind direction as possible and fly down it at traffic altitude. Establish the crab necessary to keep the airplane directly over the road and look back to clear the area.

2. Pick a point on the road and fly a circle to bring the airplane back to the starting point. Perfect flying produces a perfect circle.

3. On a perfectly calm day, you would use a medium bank throughout, producing a given circle. On windy days, try to fly approximately the same size circle, varying the bank as necessary.

4. Going upwind, for the first 180°, the bank is shallower.

5. Going downwind for the last half of the circle, the bank is steeper.

6. Complete the roll-out just as the airplane returns to the starting point on the road. Wings should return to a level position with the nose at the proper crab angle. Thus, roll-out will occur later downwind and earlier upwind.

7. Fly on down the road briefly, holding the necessary amount of crab, and fly the same size circle in the opposite direction.

### Common Errors of Student

1. Poor selection of road for maneuver because of traffic, obstructions, etc.

2. Unable to visualize pattern of the circle.

3. Gains or loses altitude or airspeed excessively.

4. Makes dangerously steep turns to correct pattern.

5. Spoils the pattern by allowing airplane to drift inside the circle upwind (bank too steep) and drift outside the circle downwind (bank too shallow).

6. Doesn't look around enough.

7. Poor timing on roll-out, failing to level off at proper crab angle over the road.

# SPIRALS

The Spiral is used for losing altitude smoothly and rapidly over a given area. It gives you practice in coordination, in correction for drift, and in control of the airplane in diving turn attitudes.

The Spiral you practice in Basic Training is an extended diving turn through 360° or more with reduced power and with airspeed held between 110 to 120 mph. A turn through 360° is a one-turn Spiral, 720° a two-turn Spiral, etc.

Spirals executed without reference to a specific landmark are relatively simple, but spirals about a given point require greater skill.

Auxiliary Controls: In cruising positions.

### Procedure

1. Clear the area, and reduce the throttle considerably, holding only enough power to keep the engine clear, and roll into a bank with the nose slightly below the horizon.

2. Hold a constant airspeed of 110 to 120 mph by back stick pressure.

3. General rule: At higher altitudes, use a steeper bank (60° to 70°) and less throttle. At lower altitudes, use a shallower bank and more throttle.

4. If you wish to lose altitude over a particular spot, vary the bank to correct for drift.

5. Continually clear the area and recover at a safe altitude.

## Common Errors of Student

1. Doesn't coordinate controls properly.
2. Allows airspeed to vary too much.
3. Holds off the bank with stick, tending to shallow the bank and produce a skid.
4. Starts the Spiral too close to the landmark, requiring too steep a bank to keep the landmark in the center of the turn.
5. Fails to anticipate wind drift, drifting away from the center point downwind and toward the center point upwind.

**Note:** The Spiral is not a precision maneuver. It can usually be learned easily and then practiced when it is necessary to lose altitude quickly.

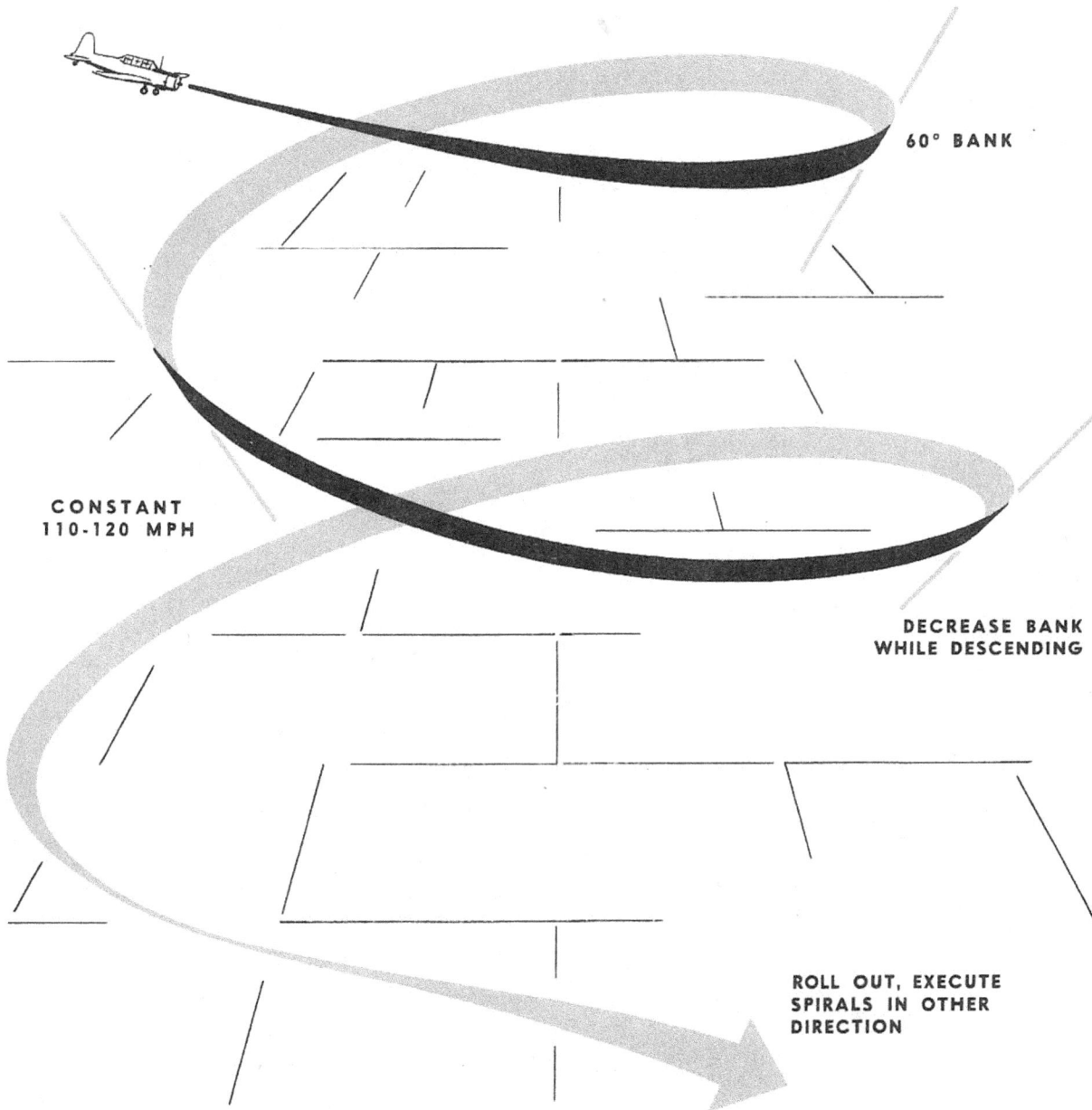

60° BANK

CONSTANT
110-120 MPH

DECREASE BANK
WHILE DESCENDING

ROLL OUT, EXECUTE
SPIRALS IN OTHER
DIRECTION

# STEEP TURNS

**65° TO 70° BANK**

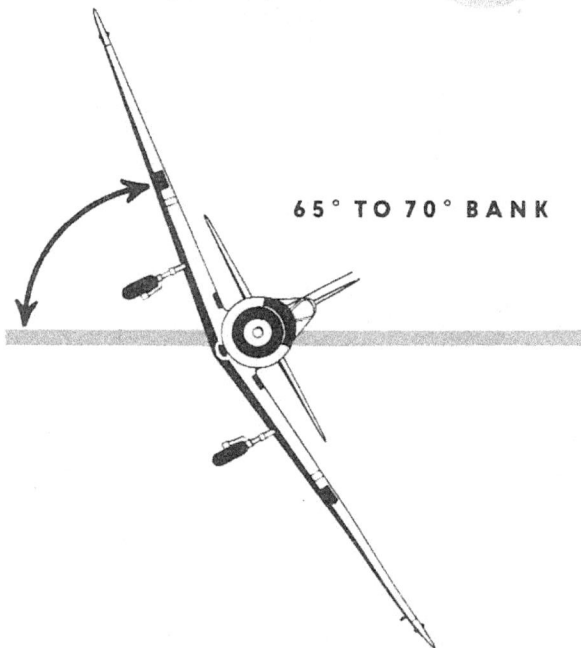

As soon as you show good coordination in medium turns, you will be given Steep Turns. They are precision, maximum performance maneuvers extremely important in combat flying!

Steep Turns are more quickly mastered if approached gradually. Usually you will start with a medium bank and make each succeeding bank steeper than the last. Later you will make all Steep Turns at not less than 60° or more than 70° of bank . . . because less than a 60° bank will not permit maximum performance and more than a 70° bank is difficult to fly smoothly.

### Points to Remember

The functions of controls never change. However, if the nose gets down, as frequently happens in Steep Turns, sufficient back pressure to raise it may cause a stall. Increased bank increases the wing loading and the stalling speed . . . a 60° bank increases the stalling speed approximately 40 per cent. If the nose is too low, it may be necessary to decrease the bank slightly while raising the nose. Then smoothly move back into the steep bank, precisely coordinating back pressure, rudder, and ailerons, to hold the nose on the horizon.

Don't try to make corrections with rudder alone, back pressure alone, or ailerons alone. Always use stick and rudder together in turns.

Keep looking around during Steep Turns. Glance from the altimeter to the position of the nose to the angle of bank on the horizon, etc.

Auxiliary Controls: In cruising position except throttle advanced to 2,000 rpm.

### Procedure

1. Pick out a section line or straight road, line up with it, advance the throttle to 2,000 rpm, re-trim the airplane, and clear the area by looking past the tail.

2. Roll smoothly into the turn, using firm, continuous pressures on stick and rudder until you reach the desired degree of bank. As the bank increases, the nose should move more and more rapidly along the horizon.

3. Maintain the bank until near the 180° point. Then roll out smoothly so that wings are level just as you reach the 180° point. Check with your reference line.

4. In early practice roll out to straight and level flight after each turn. Later roll from one Steep Turn directly into another.

### Common Errors of Student

1. Attempts to control the position of the nose with top rudder alone.

2. Tends to roll into the turn with aileron and rudder alone, without coordinating back pressure.

3. Rough movement of controls.

4. Applies excessive back pressure, causing airplane to mush or stall.

5. Fails to maintain a constant bank and constant rate of turn.

6. Incorrect throttle setting.

7. Poor coordination, resulting in slips and skids.

8. Fails to trim airplane for increased throttle setting.

9. Overshoots or undershoots the 180° point.

10. Fails to maintain a constant altitude.

11. Fails to clear the area by looking around.

# MAXIMUM PERFORMANCE

## Climbing Turns

This maneuver is the connecting link between the approach to a stall and a chandelle. In the approach to a stall, you learn to pull directly into the desired attitude in one smooth motion, hold it, and at the last moment roll out. In the Maximum Performance Climbing Turn, the attitude of the airplane is **constantly changing**. The nose continues to rise **gradually** throughout the maneuver, and the bank changes **gradually** from level flight to approximately a medium bank and then back to level flight just as the airplane reaches the maximum angle of climb. In effect, the nose draws a straight line up from the horizon in the direction of the turn.

This maneuver differs from the chandelle in that no definite amount of turn is required. The important thing is proper timing for maximum performance and a uniform,

**gradual** change of attitude. Get this down pat and you will have no difficulty with chandelles.

Auxiliary Controls: In cruising positions.

### Procedure

1. Clear the area by looking back in the direction of the turn. Start the maneuver from straight and level flight, cruising airspeed.

2. Blend rudder, aileron, and back pressure simultaneously to start a gradual climbing turn. Don't establish a turn and then pull up into a climb.

3. **Gradually** increase both the angle of climb and the angle of bank for approximately two-thirds of the maneuver. Continue to increase the climb but **gradually** reduce the bank so that wings are level again just as you reach the maximum climbing attitude.

4. Hesitate for an instant on the verge of a stall, to check this maximum climbing atti-

tude, and then lower the nose smoothly to the horizon.

5. Hesitate again briefly, and then use a shallow dive to regain cruising speed. Level off at cruising airspeed before starting the next maneuver.

### Common Errors of Student

1. Banks before establishing the climb instead of blending the two.

2. Uses too much climb and too little turn, resulting in a high unbalanced maneuver, or vice versa.

3. Fails to vary amount of torque correction as airspeed decreases.

4. Completes maneuver before maximum performance is reached.

5. Prolongs maneuver into a stall.

6. Uses poor timing so that the roll-out must be hurried to prevent a stall.

7. Fails to clear the area before starting the climbing turn.

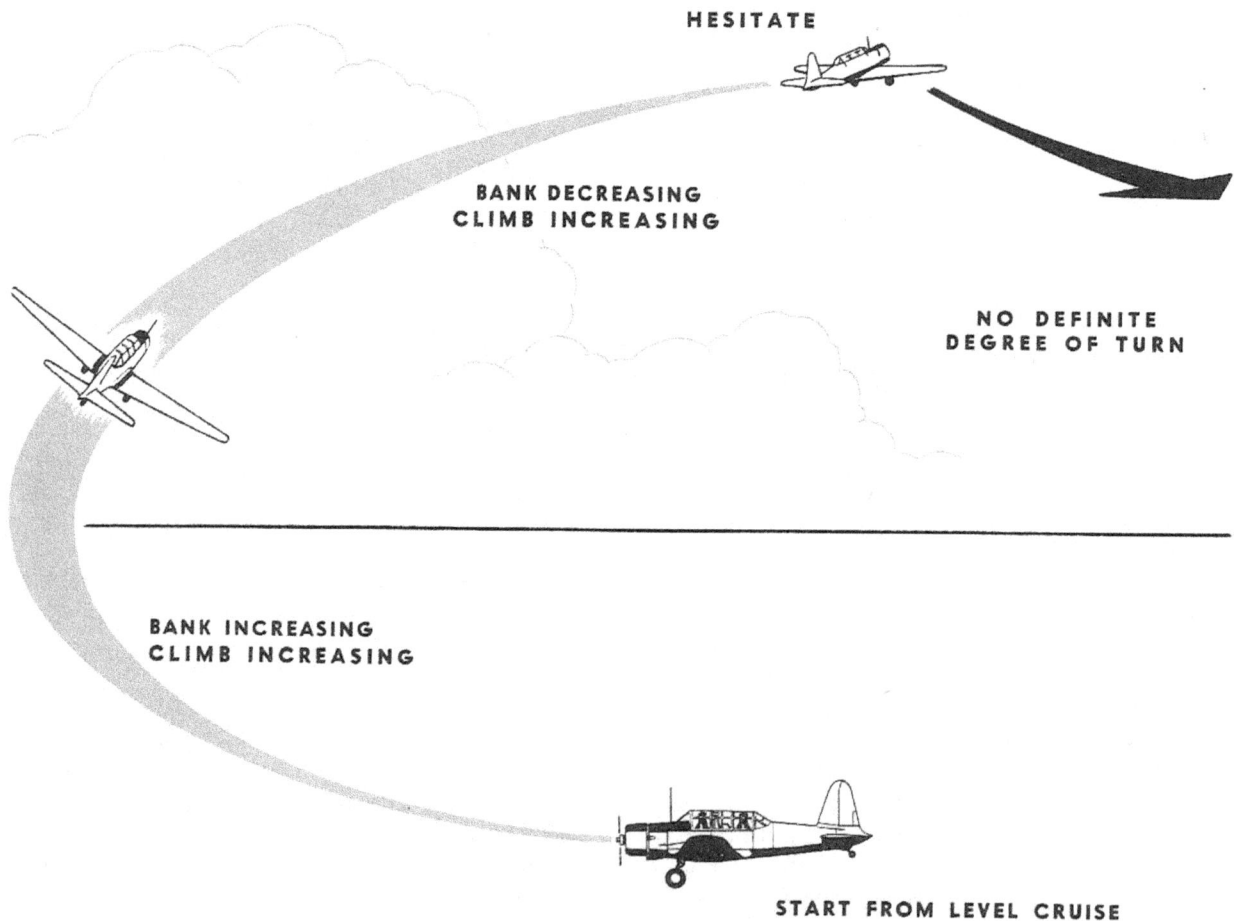

HESITATE

BANK DECREASING
CLIMB INCREASING

NO DEFINITE
DEGREE OF TURN

BANK INCREASING
CLIMB INCREASING

START FROM LEVEL CRUISE

# Chandelles

The Chandelle is a composite maneuver combining a shallow dive, a coordinated maximum performance climbing turn, and a precision roll-out. The Chandelle is a precision maneuver executed through 180° of turn. There are many types of Chandelles, but your first job is to master the standard training Chandelle specified in Basic training. When you can do it perfectly, then you can experiment with others.

Polish up your technique in maximum performance climbing turns before trying Chandelles. The two are very similar except that the Chandelle is entered from a shallow dive, at higher airspeed, and must be timed for exactly 180° of turn.

Learn all you possibly can from your instructor. You get less and less dual time as the course progresses. Listen hard, ask questions, and make the most of your time in the air and on the flight line.

Auxiliary Controls: In cruising positions.

## Procedure

1. Line up on a road or section line and fly along it. Clear the area by looking back past the tail in the direction of the turn. Lower the nose into a shallow dive and hold it until your airspeed reaches approximately 140 mph.

2. Start a climbing turn, steadily increasing the angle of bank and the angle of climb

HESITATE

CRUISING THROTTLE

*HERE WE GO AGAIN!*

exactly as in a maximum performance climbing turn.

3. At approximately 135° to the original flight path (or three-quarters of the way through the maneuver), the bank will be near vertical, but never past.

4. Now continue to **increase** the angle of climb but **gradually decrease** the angle of bank.

5. Properly executed, you will complete 180° of turn just as you reach minimum airspeed and maximum angle of climb (approximately 40°), and just as the wings roll out level.

6. Hesitate briefly, with the nose straight ahead, to check the reference line and climb-

ing attitude; then lower the nose smoothly to the horizon to prevent a stall.

7. If you are about to stall while rolling out, lower the nose enough to prevent the stall.

### Torque

The perfect pattern for this Chandelle requires a constant rate of turn of the nose, a constant rise of the nose, carefully timed increase and decrease of bank, and a precision roll-out at the 180° point.

The most difficult part of the Chandelle is torque correction, which varies throughout the maneuver. In a Chandelle to the right, torque comes into play soon after you start

180° OF TURN

140 MPH

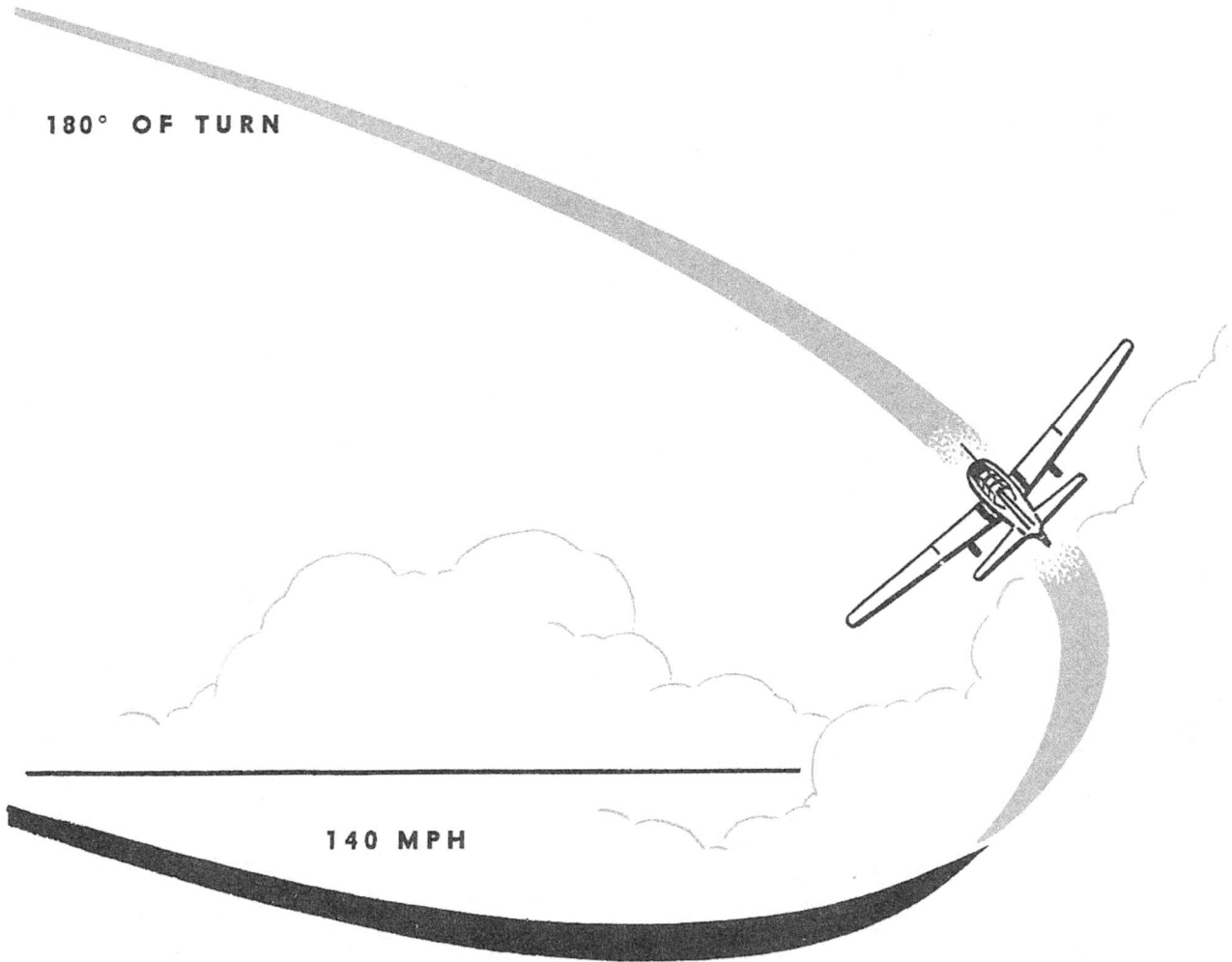

the climbing turn and increases as flying speed decreases. Torque is at a maximum during the roll-out.

In a Chandelle to the left, use minimum aileron pressure but considerable right rudder pressure in the roll-out to overcome torque and to stop the turn. In a Chandelle to the right, you need much less rudder pressure in the roll-out but more aileron pressure.

## Common Errors of Student

1. Does not clear the area.
2. Dives improperly, using inconsistent airspeed in pull-ups, and fails to start bank and climb together.
3. Steepens the original bank too rapidly, resulting in nothing more than a steep bank with the nose pulled up rapidly at end of the turn.
4. Keeps bank too shallow but raises nose steadily, resulting in a stall before the turn is completed.
5. Raises nose too high too quickly instead of raising it gradually throughout 180° of turn.
6. Fails to blend movements of controls.
7. Fails to correct for torque, particularly during roll-out.
8. Fails to hesitate briefly after the roll-out to check attitude.
9. Falls short of or turns in excess of 180°.

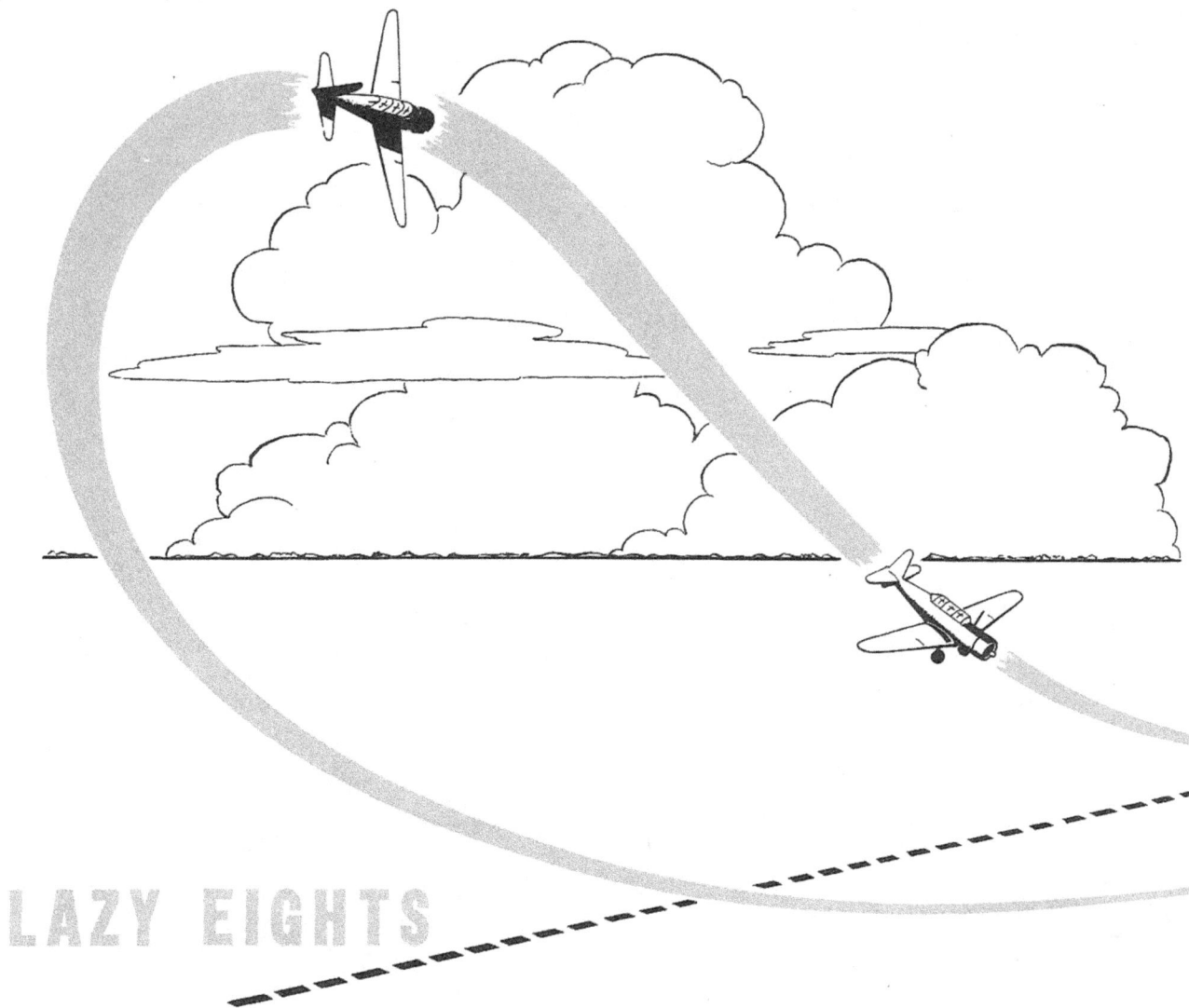

# LAZY EIGHTS

The pilot who can do consistently good Lazy Eights is on his way to the big leagues.

Lazy Eights require the utmost in timing, control touch, and orientation. The airplane must go from climbing turns to diving turns smoothly, without stalling, without developing excessive diving speed, and while maintaining a constant rate of turn.

Although there are many varieties, one particular Lazy Eight is taught in Basic Schools to avoid confusion. It is to the student's advantage to learn it well.

## Pattern

The flight path of the airplane is not actually that of a figure eight. However, the pilot has the feeling in flight that he is executing an eight, because the nose of the airplane describes equal arcs above and below the horizon.

The pilot flies the airplane smoothly and gradually from climbing turns into diving turns, to produce a rounded, lazy maneuver. The maneuver is started from straight and level flight with one running light on the reference point. The pilot executes a climbing turn with bank and climb gradually increasing.

From the maximum point of climb he flies the nose slowly down through the reference point, and times his change of attitude in the diving turn so that the airplane will momen-

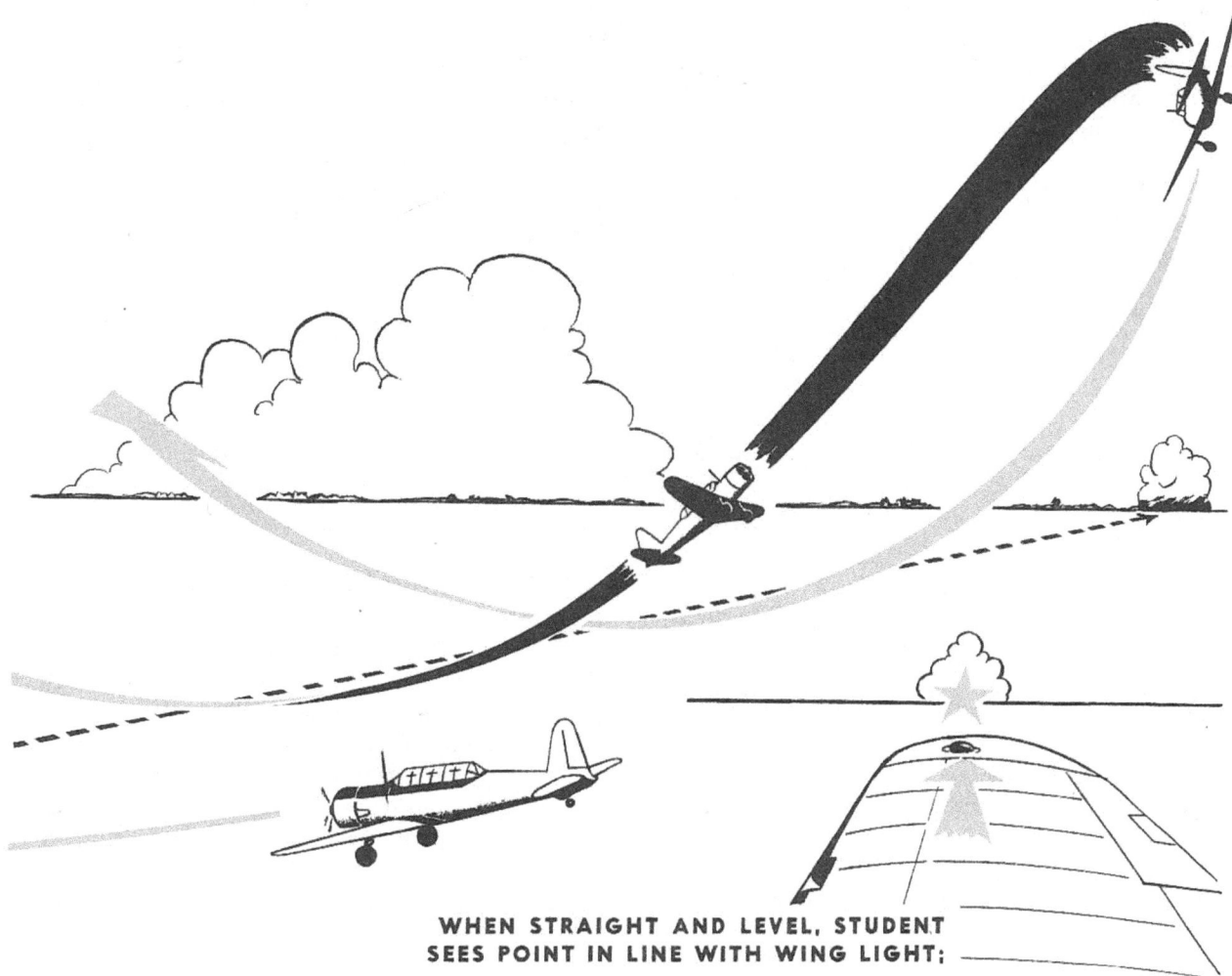

WHEN STRAIGHT AND LEVEL, STUDENT
SEES POINT IN LINE WITH WING LIGHT;

tarily return to straight and level flight just as the opposite running light is lined up with the reference point. Smoothly, without hesitation, he starts a similar pattern in the opposite direction.

The object is to produce a steady, lazy, rounded pattern in which the attitude of the airplane never stops changing, but all of the changes are gradual—lazy!

Auxiliary Controls: In cruising positions.

## Procedure

1.  Select a reference point on the horizon, such as a hill or smokestack, and maneuver the airplane 90° to this point so that you see one running light on the point.

2.  Be sure the area is clear and, from level flight and cruising airspeed, start a gentle climbing turn.

3.  Gradually increase bank and climb so that when the airplane has turned 45° the nose will be approximately 40° above the horizon, the wings banked approximately 45° and flying speed just below a stall. This is the top of one arc of the 8.

4.  Then bring the nose lazily down through the reference point into a lazy dive, forming an arc below the horizon about equal to the one above. Continue the turn as you gradually raise the nose and level the wings.

5.  When you have completed 180° of turn you should have the nose back on the horizon,

airspeed back at cruising (approximately 130 mph), running light on the horizon reference point, and the same altitude as when the maneuver began.

6. Don't hesitate in level flight. Start the same maneuver in the opposite direction to complete the last half of the figure 8.

### Common Errors of Student

1. Fails to use reference point properly.
2. Fails to establish bank and turn together and time the turn correctly.
3. Banks (or climbs) too steeply instead of gradually increasing the bank (or climb).

4. Tends to slip when approaching the maximum climb from left to right. (More bottom rudder will prevent this but is not needed when going from right to left.)
5. Fails to fly the nose through the point or covers the point with the nose. (It is more accurate to pick a spot on the engine cowling and put it through the reference point.)
6. Dives too steeply, building up too much airspeed.
7. Rolls out, pulls nose up, and then rolls into the next turn. (To make loops of the 8 rounded, roll out of one diving turn directly into the next climbing turn.)

# ADVANCED FORCED LANDINGS

You will practice Simulated Forced Landings during **every dual transition ride** throughout the course, but **never** solo. Your knowledge of wind direction and velocity, judgment in selecting fields, and technique in executing Forced Landings must show constant improvement.

At the end of 50 hours you should be hitting fields with consistent regularity, and you can expect your forced landings to get increasingly difficult. Your instructor will stage them in locations where the choice of fields is poor, where the approach pattern is more

difficult, where exceptional judgment is necessary in deciding whether to simulate landing crosswind or not, where the field is at maximum gliding distance away, or where quick reactions are necessary to get into the best available field.

You may go years or forever without having to make an actual forced landing. However, most peace-time pilots have had a forced landing at one time or another. In combat there is a much greater chance you will need such skill. Learn all you can and be safe. Store up skill now for the future.

# DRAGGING STRANGE FIELDS

HMM GOPHERS.

You are in strange country, have completely lost your bearings, night is approaching, your radio is "out," and your fuel is running low. You decide that there are some decent fields near and that you had better land. Your next logical move is to drag a field.

Dragging a field allows the pilot to examine it closely for obstacles, to decide on the best approach, and to make certain that it is a suitable landing area. You may drag several fields before you find a suitable one. Be sure you know how to do this before you start cross country flying.

## Procedure

1. Determine the wind direction, select the best available field and circle it at 500 ft. to choose the best approach and the best landing strip. **Look closely for all obstacles** both on the approach and exit from the field. Choose another field if there are obstructions in your flight path.

2. Move propeller control forward to High rpm, reduce airspeed below 120 mph, lower flaps (20° on Vultee Trainer), lose altitude in a wide circle, and approach the field into the wind at 50 to 75 ft. above the ground.

3. Fly across the field at approximately 100 mph. a little to one side of the strip selected for landing.

4. Examine the field closely for rocks, stumps, ditches, soft muddy spots, etc.

5. After you have passed over the field, decide whether you would have landed there. Check with your instructor. Find out if he saw hazards that you didn't see.

## Warning:

Don't be a Kiwi Bird! (Flies backward because he doesn't care where he's going but wants to see where he's been.) Don't look backwards to check the field. **Watch out for obstructions ahead.** Never land in strange fields except in actual emergencies or unless specifically authorized to do so.

This is a relatively dangerous maneuver and must be done with extreme care. As a last resort, you can use it to orient yourself if you are lost. The names of towns are almost always painted on both ends of the railroad station in large letters. The object is to fly by the station and read the name of the town. Your instructor will explain and demonstrate how this is done.

### Procedure

1. Circle the town at about 1,000 ft. while spotting all tall buildings, church steeples, high tension wires, and other obstructions.

2. Scan water tanks and buildings for possible identification of the town, and plan your approach.

3. Move propeller control forward to High rpm, reduce airspeed below 120 mph, lower 20° of flaps (on Vultee Type Trainer), and lose altitude while getting into position for the approach.

4. The best approach is usually parallel to the tracks at about 75 ft. and as close to the station as possible. If tall obstructions make this hazardous, approach the station perpendicular to the tracks. Make a power-on approach at a good safe speed of 100 mph or more.

5. Keep shifting your eyes. Don't concentrate all your attention on the station. Fly the airplane, look at the town, watch out for obstacles.

6. One glance at the station as you go by is usually enough to read the name of the town.

## Warning:

This maneuver is taught for your own protection. It will be demonstrated only at points selected and approved by the Director of Training, after permission has been secured from the town authorities. Practice "shooting" of stations without authority will be severely punished. **Never shoot a railroad station on a solo flight except in an actual emergency.**

# Solo Spins

Spins start early in Basic Training and you will practice one or more during every dual transition flight throughout the entire course.

After approximately 35 hours, you should be expert in executing and recovering from spins. Then Solo Spins will be scheduled.

Shortly before Solo Spins begin, review all the important points in spin entries and recoveries. (See "Spins" on P. 63-64-65.)

### Required

After 50 hours, two 3-turn Solo Spins will be scheduled. Remember that three turns is the **maximum** authorized in Basic Training and that more turns are a waste of time and altitude.

Don't be one of those wise guys who wants to see what happens in a 5-turn or 6-turn spin. Remember that the spin sometimes tightens up after the third turn and that too many turns can make you dangerously dizzy.

KEEP CALM — AND TAKE YOUR TIME!

# SOLO ACCURACY STAGES

In accuracy stages you go on your own in competition with others who have about the same amount of training that you have. Solo accuracy stages are not merely check rides. The object is to give you more practice so you can develop greater accuracy in various types of landings.

Don't let your instructor down. Your performance will reflect on him so do your darndest! Review all you have learned in dual and solo flights and read what this manual has to say about the stage that is scheduled.

One of the instructors or a control officer will be running each stage and grading you.

Try to turn in a good performance during every stage. Here is an opportunity to perfect your judgment and technique. It's your chance to benefit from the suggestions of the control officer.

If you loaf through the stages, if you take a know-it-all attitude, or if you try to just get by, you aren't fooling anyone but yourself. Soon you'll be flying a more high-powered airplane all by your lonesome and you'll be thankful for everything you've learned.

For the convenience of the student, the most important points concerning each stage are given in the pages that follow.

# LANDING STAGES IN BASIC SCHOOLS

90 DEGREE ACCURACY STAGE – POWER OFF
90 DEGREE POWER APPROACH STAGE
CROSSWIND STAGE
HURDLE STAGE

# 90 DEGREE ACCURACY STAGE (POWER OFF)

## (TOTAL MINIMUM OF 15 SATISFACTORY LANDINGS IN TWO STAGES ON DIFFERENT DAYS)

This consists of landing practice from a 90° side approach with the emphasis on accuracy—good take-offs, proper traffic pattern, smooth turns, correct setting of the base leg, throttle cut at the right time, uniform glides, and precision landings. Here are pointers that will help you turn in a better performance.

### Take-Off

Controls: Propeller control forward in high rpm (keep it there all the time when going around on successive landings); flaps down 20° during take-off and in traffic (on Vultee Trainer).

Make sure no airplanes are on the approach as you taxi into take-off position. Delay take-off until the airplane ahead has started into its first turn to assure safe spacing between airplanes.

### Traffic Pattern

Traffic should proceed around the field in a rectangular pattern at 700 ft. above the ground. Keep a lookout for other airplanes, make definite turns with medium banks, and be as careful about correct flying in traffic as about the landing itself. Airspeed for traffic is normally 105 to 110 mph. The downwind leg must be far enough out from the field so that it isn't necessary to cut the throttle in a hurry after turning on the base leg.

There are five things to keep in mind when shooting accuracy landings: altitude, airspeed, effect of wind, location of the base leg, and location of the key point.

### Base Leg and Key Point

Don't make the mistake of putting your base leg too far out from the field so that

I THINK I'M GONNA MAKE IT!

# ACCURACY CONTROL

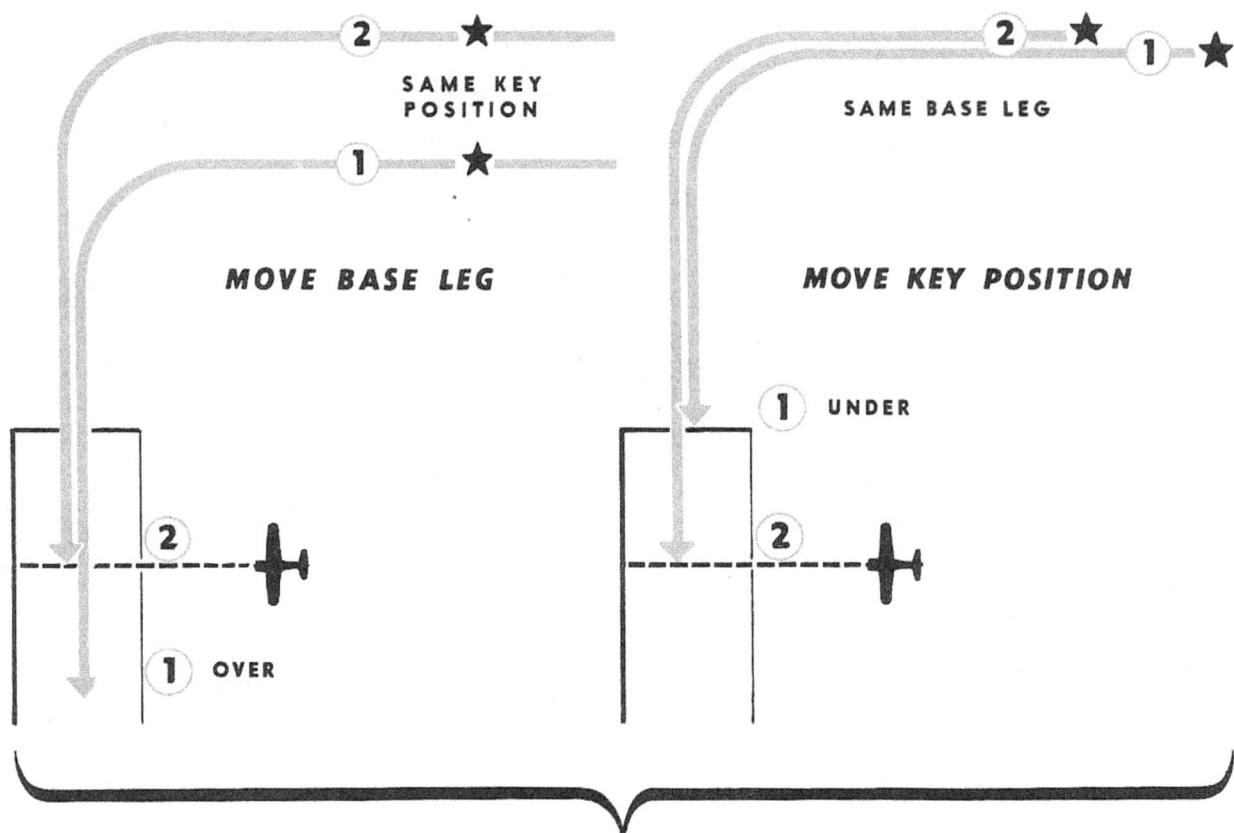

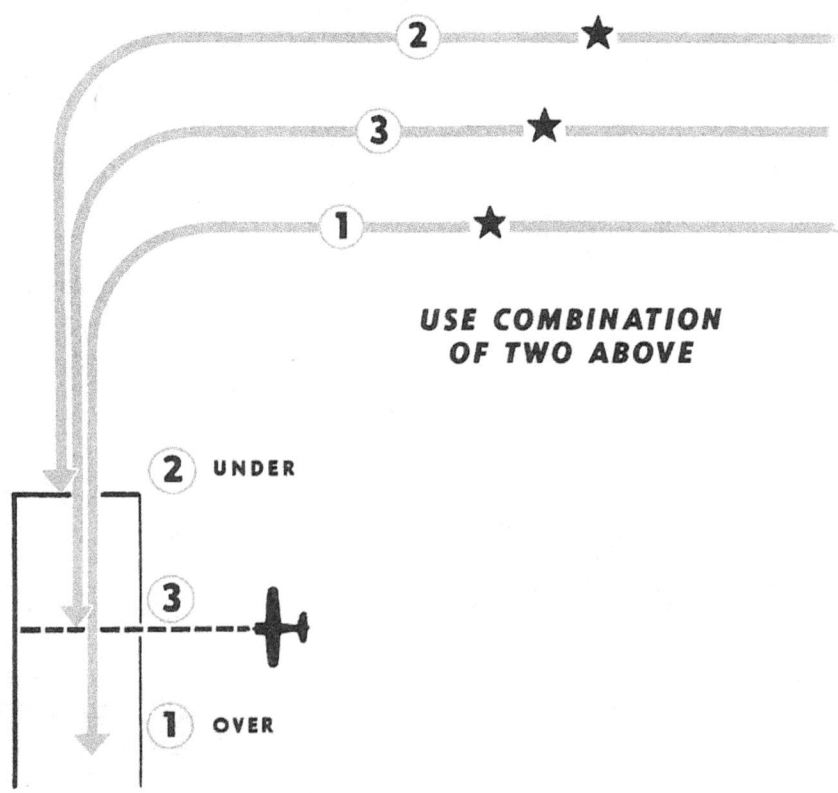

2 ★

SAME KEY
POSITION

1 ★

**MOVE BASE LEG**

2 ★ 1 ★

SAME BASE LEG

**MOVE KEY POSITION**

1 UNDER

2

2

1 OVER

2 ★

3 ★

1 ★

**USE COMBINATION
OF TWO ABOVE**

2 UNDER

3

1 OVER

your turn on final approach comes immediately after you cut the throttle before there is time to establish a normal glide. As a general guide, you can fix the Key Point at an angle of 45° from the point where you intend to land.

The supervisor of the stage will usually require you to land in the first third of the field along some definite strip or between markers. At most fields the general practice is to mark off a runway with cloth panels, because future training will be on runways and because runway landings require greater accuracy than landings anywhere along the width of a sod field.

### Think Ahead of the Airplane

Think ahead of the airplane all the time. Pick a definite approach lane and a definite landing spot and cut your throttle to bring you in according to plan. Then you can see your own mistakes and will know how to correct them.

After you cut the throttle, wait until your speed is approximately 90 mph, lower the nose to gliding position, and re-trim. Hold a smooth, even glide with the nose at a steady angle below the horizon. Don't drop the nose too much in the gliding turn and remember: **low turns will not be tolerated.**

In a field without runways, you can come in anywhere along the width of the field. If you cut the throttle too early on the base leg, you will have to land in a nearer lane; if you cut the throttle too late, you can continue the base leg to a turn into a farther lane. In each case the turn should be made at approximately the same, safe altitude. This is approved procedure provided you will shoot for a definite landing strip and note the error which causes you to fall short or go past it. **Flaps:** In the first stage use a set amount of flaps (probably 40°) to detect errors in fixing the key point.

The second stage should include various settings up to full flaps. Use the proper gliding angles for different flap settings; and don't get in the habit of gliding too fast and then using flaps to kill the excess speed. This is poor technique.

### The Landing

Execute the landing itself normally. If the base leg, key point, and glide are correct, the landing itself nearly always comes off smoothly. You will learn a lot from the suggestions and criticisms of the supervisor of the stage.

### Don't Repeat Errors

Never make the same mistake twice. If you overshoot on the first approach, make a **definite** correction. It is better to undershoot slightly on the second approach than to correct only partially for overshooting. One overshooting approach followed by an undershooting approach ("bracketing") gives you the key to the right middle path. Spot the position of your base leg and the location of your key point. You must know where they were in order to change them.

Remember that strong wind will require a base leg closer in and throttle cut a little later than when there is little or no wind. Learn to anticipate and correct for wind before it causes you to undershoot.

### Changing the Approach

If you are overshooting or undershooting, you may need to change your approach. One way is to move the key point forward or back along the base leg; another is to establish the base leg nearer or farther from the field. Use a combination of these two. If overshooting, move the base leg out a little and the key point back a little; and reverse the procedure if you are undershooting. Review overshooting and undershooting procedures.

### Common Errors of Student

1. Flies an irregular traffic pattern.
2. Makes dangerously low turns.
3. Sets base leg too close in (or too far out).
4. Doesn't use good judgment in selecting key point.
5. Glides erratically (or too fast, or too slowly).
6. Repeatedly overshoots or undershoots.
7. Doesn't correct key point and base leg.
8. Doesn't shoot for a definite landing spot.
9. Handles airplane roughly in roundout.
10. Makes wheels-first or tail-first landings.
11. Consistently repeats same error.

# 90 DEGREE POWER APPROACH

## (MINIMUM OF SIX SATISFACTORY LANDINGS)

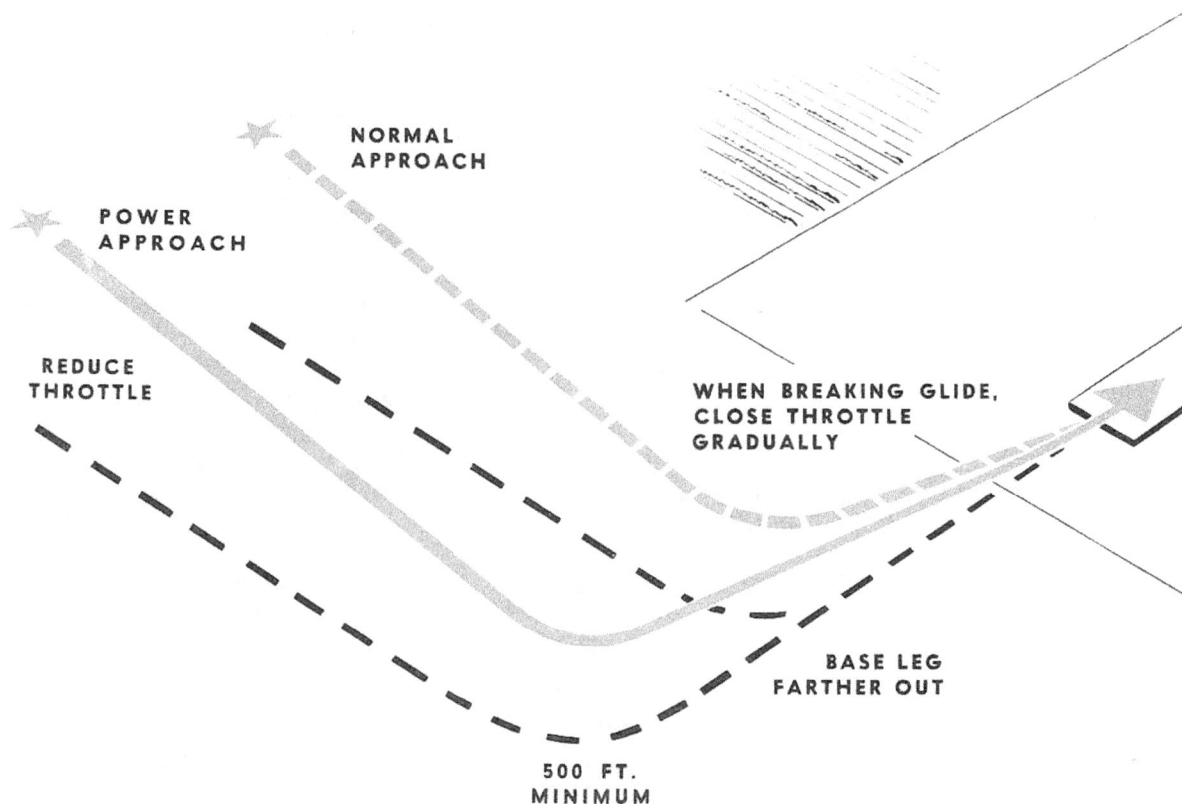

NORMAL
APPROACH

POWER
APPROACH

REDUCE
THROTTLE

WHEN BREAKING GLIDE,
CLOSE THROTTLE
GRADUALLY

BASE LEG
FARTHER OUT

500 FT.
MINIMUM

All landings at strange fields are made with a Power-On Approach. Accuracy developed in this stage also will be immediately helpful in night flying and cross country navigation flights.

### Technique

This approach is similar to the normal 90° side approach except for the following:

1. Set the base leg 50 percent farther out from the field than in a power-off approach.

2. Reduce throttle substantially at the key point and dissipate your airspeed.

3. Start the turn into final approach with a safe margin of airspeed and at a safe altitude—**never lower than** 500 ft.

4. On the final approach, roll down additional flaps, if needed. Normally you will establish a shallower glide than usual and then achieve a constant rate of descent to the desired landing spot by adjustments of throttle. The more throttle used, the shallower the glide angle.

5. As you begin to break your glide, start to retard the throttle so that it is fully back just before you contact the ground.

6. Adjust flaps to the situation, but in a strong crosswind use a minimum of flaps.

# CROSSWIND STAGE

The pilot who knows how, can bring a skittish airplane in crosswind with no difficulty. The Basic Trainer is a stable airplane with a wide tread and is relatively easy to land crosswind. Perfect your technique on this airplane and you'll have much less difficulty with more high-powered ones.

## Effect of Crosswind

It is helpful to know the effect of a crosswind on the airplane during a landing:

1. Pressure builds up under the upwind wing, tending to raise that wing.

2. The fuselage blankets out the downwind side of the airplane, tending to drop the downwind wing so that the airplane wants to tip over away from the wind.

3. The nose wants to turn into the wind because the weight is principally on the front wheels. The wind trys to blow the tail around and to ground-loop the airplane into the wind.

4. Flaps increase these tendencies. The more flaps and the stronger the wind, the more the airplane wants to have its own way.

Proper technique permits perfectly safe Crosswind Landings. The three different methods of approach most commonly used are the crabbing approach, the slipping approach, and the combination approach.

## Crabbing Approach

Head the airplane into the wind enough to make a track along the ground in line with the landing strip, and enough to keep the airplane from drifting with the wind. Just before you contact the ground, use rudder to line up with the landing lane and ailerons as necessary to keep the wings level.

Don't remove the crab too soon or the airplane will start to drift with the wind.

## Slipping Approach

In this approach the object is to slip the airplane into the wind sufficiently to offset the drifting action of the wind so that the airplane will make a straight track along the ground parallel to the landing lane.

Drop the upwind wing and hold it down at the proper angle with ailerons. Hold the airplane parallel to the landing lane with the rudder.

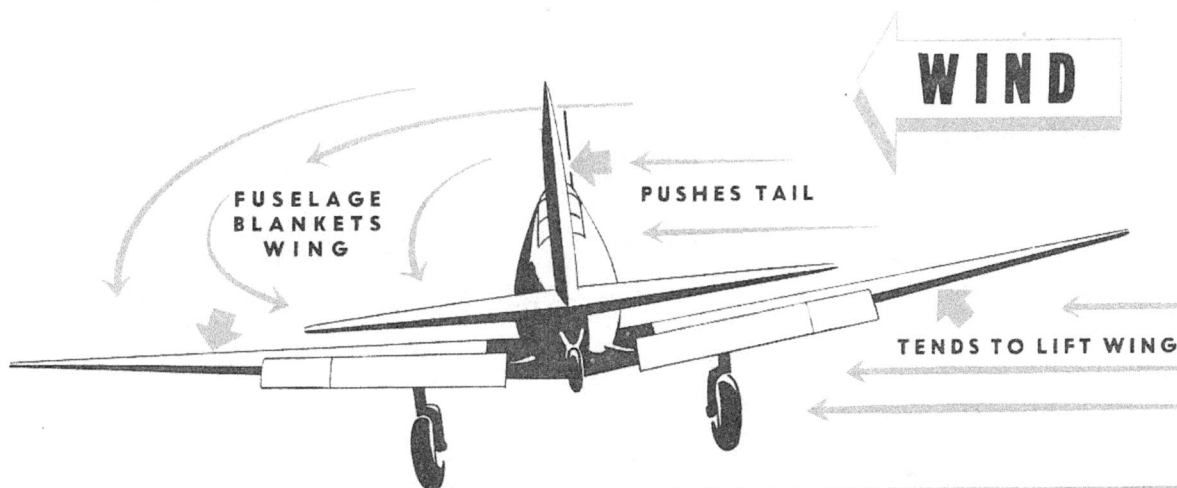

WIND

FUSELAGE BLANKETS WING

PUSHES TAIL

TENDS TO LIFT WING

# CORRECTING FOR CROSSWIND

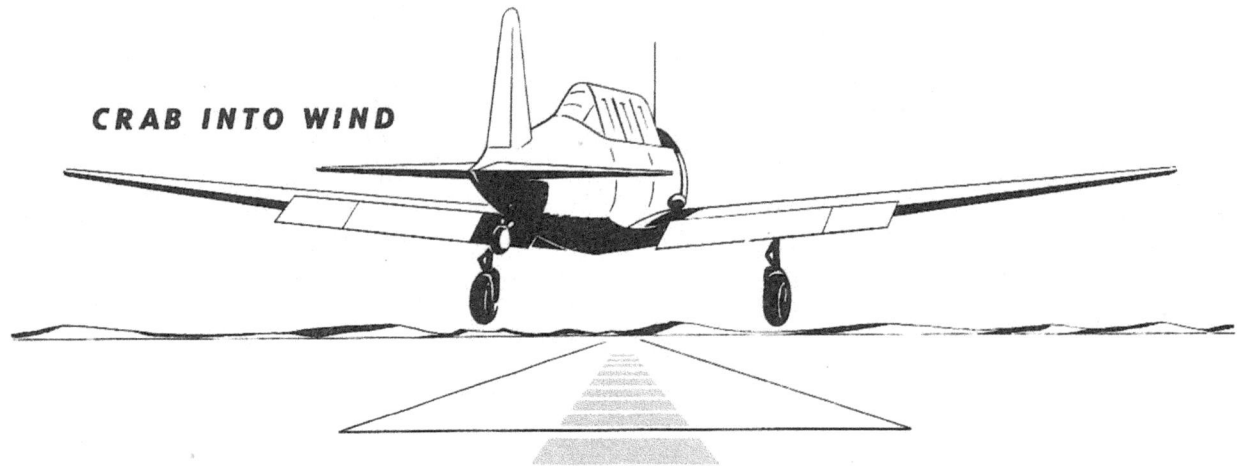

WIND

SLIP INTO WIND

CRAB INTO WIND

COMBINATION OF BOTH
SLIP AND CRAB IS BEST

94

Just before contacting the ground, raise the wing to level position with the ailerons and keep the airplane lined up with the landing lane with rudder control.

Don't stop slipping too soon or the airplane will start to drift with the wind again. Remove the slip at the last moment before landing.

### Combination Approach

This is simply a combination of the crabbing and slipping approaches. It requires less crabbing than the crabbing method and less slipping than the slipping method to accomplish the same result. The advantage is obvious . . . the attitude of the airplane can be corrected more quickly and easily just before landing than in the all-crab or all-slip approaches. The Combination Approach is the safest and best of the three, particularly for larger aircraft.

### Landing Roll

During the first part of the landing roll, speed helps to maintain rudder control. Most ground loops occur toward the end of the roll when students are tempted to pump or fan opposite rudder. This can disengage the tail-wheel and cause it to swivel free. Then the airplane is almost certain to go out of control. Here is the approved procedure for the landing roll:

1. Hold the stick all the way back, and hold the airplane straight ahead with the rudder.

2. As speed decreases, **don't over-control** with the rudder. Instead, if necessary, use a **slight amount** of brake with rudder, applying and releasing brakes to bring the airplane back to a straight ahead track.

3. The time to stop a ground loop is **before it starts**. It's much easier to **hold the airplane straight** than to bring it back after it starts to veer.

### Crosswind Take-Off

The most important thing in a crosswind take-off is to hold the airplane directly on a point straight ahead. Also keep it on the ground a little longer than usual to be sure that it will stay up when it does take off. A bouncing take-off in a crosswind puts too much strain on the landing gear. As soon as you are off, establish a crab angle to hold to the original ground track.

### Common Errors of Student

1. Uses insufficient crab or slip.

2. Breaks crab or slip too soon so the airplane starts to drift.

3. Lands without neutralizing drift correction.

4. Is unable to combine crab and slip properly.

5. Doesn't hold the airplane straight during the roll.

6. Fans and pumps the rudder excessively.

7. Doesn't use brakes when he should.

# HURDLE STAGE

### (TOTAL MINIMUM OF 12 LANDINGS DURING TWO SATISFACTORY STAGES ON DIFFERENT DAYS)

The object of Hurdle practice is to teach students how to come in over an obstacle and bring the wheels solidly to the ground within a minimum distance from the hurdle. This requires maximum performance precision flying. The practical value of Hurdle Landings is vividly demonstrated day after day in combat areas when planes must come in to half-demolished fields, land on short strips of beach over tall trees, or execute emergency forced landings in limited space. Good Hurdle Landings have saved many a pilot and crew.

The approach is made over a 16-ft. hurdle consisting of a rope stretched between two standards 100 ft. apart. Usually the standard is constructed so that it will tip down if the tail strikes the rope, but it is wise to clear the hurdle. A tree or a hangar won't drop down for you if you come in too low.

### Technique

Hurdle Landings require a special technique entirely different from normal landings. The airplane must be at a higher altitude on the final approach, the attitude is different, and airspeed will be between 75 and 80 mph (in BT-13A). Here is a point-by-point description of good hurdle technique:

1. Set the base leg about one-fourth farther from the field than in a normal landing.

2. Retard the throttle on the base leg to make the turn on final approach at about 600 ft., under partial power (90 mph), with the nose slightly lower than in level flight. This provides plenty of distance and altitude in which to get set on the final approach.

3. Immediately after the turn, lower full flaps and slow up to 75 to 80 mph, establishing a near landing attitude.

4. Use the throttle to control overshooting or undershooting. More throttle will pull the airplane in closer to the field while you still have altitude.

5. Perfectly executed, this will bring the airplane in from a high approach, at a constant rate of descent, down a relatively steep angle, barely clearing the hurdle.

6. Retard the throttle slowly and cut it entirely just before you cross the hurdle. Bring the stick back smoothly so that it reaches the full back position an instant before the wheels touch the ground.

Result: A landing that comprises three maximum performance elements: maximum rate of descent, minimum forward speed, and a minimum change of attitude in the round-out just before landing. This technique will land the airplane a minimum distance from the hurdle.

### Common Errors of Student

1. Doesn't establish steep enough flight path.

2. Builds up excessive (or insufficient) airspeed on final approach.

3. Doesn't hold a constant rate of descent.

4. Comes in low and flat and drops in (or floats).

5. Overshoots.

6. Undershoots.

### Warning:

Don't rely too much on airspeed. The feel of the controls should tell you how close you are to a stall. If the rate of descent gets too rapid or the airplane seems to be getting out of control, **give it full throttle IMMEDIATELY** to regain control! Don't let a stall develop. If you apply full throttle suddenly, use sufficient forward stick to keep the nose down and re-adjust trim tabs to prevent a stabilizer stall.

Make control movements smooth . . . never abrupt! Sudden fanning of controls tends to stall the airplane.

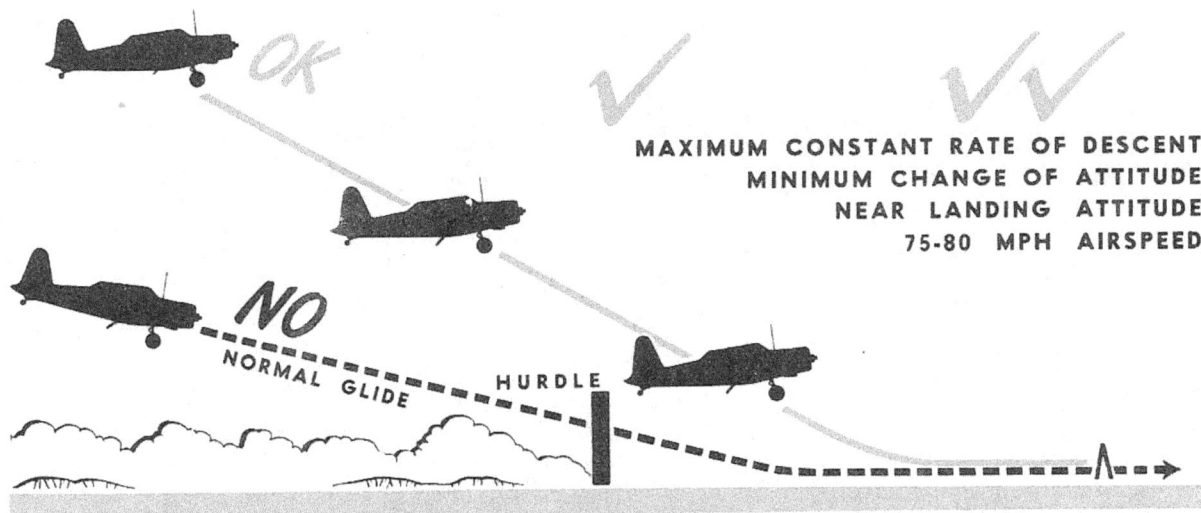

OK

MAXIMUM CONSTANT RATE OF DESCENT
MINIMUM CHANGE OF ATTITUDE
NEAR LANDING ATTITUDE
75-80 MPH AIRSPEED

NO

NORMAL GLIDE     HURDLE

# Acrobatics

CLEAR THE AREA!

Acrobatics in Basic Training consist of Loops, Snap Rolls, Slow Rolls, Half Rolls and Reverse, and Immelmann Turns. Acrobatics are a lot of fun. You get a chance to fly the airplane at higher speeds through intricate patterns. However, they have a very practical purpose—to make you feel at home in the airplane regardless of its attitude.

Acrobatics show you how to orient yourself instantly if the airplane snaps, suddenly flips on its back, or tries some other unexpected antic. But you have to apply yourself to learn all that acrobatics can teach you about flying. Construct a clear mental picture of the maneuver, and try to see and understand more and more each successive time you do it.

Don't get one-sided. Do as many rolls to the right as you do to the left and don't let one or two maneuvers run your life. Practice them all and, if anything, spend extra time on those you don't like or find difficult. Don't cheat yourself out of the varied practice that will give you all-around precision skill.

## Maximum Performance

If you use your acrobatic hours to best advantage, they will teach you much about maximum performance that will help you to perfect combat techniques. In dog-fights with the enemy you'll find yourself calling upon the airplane to do all kinds of strange things, and your own knowledge of acrobatics will help you to understand and analyze the enemy's maneuvers.

## Stay Smart

Some airplanes can take considerable punishment and some simply aren't built that way. Basic training planes are built for acrobatics and can "take it" up to a given point. You have a good margin of safety if you perform acrobatics as directed in the procedures. But don't be a "slapdamnfool" and try them too close to the ground, at excessive airspeeds, over forbidden areas, or without properly clearing the area. You can run into the ground or tear the wings off any airplane if you try hard enough. Practice acrobatics at the specified time and place.

## The Law

Terminate all acrobatics at an altitude of 5,000 ft. above the ground or higher. This is the Law! Try a Slow Roll or an Immelmann over a town some time if you want to get fired out of the Air Forces like a shot.

# LOOP

You will catch onto Loops in no time. You may feel a little squashed down in the pull-up the first few times, but so does everyone else. Try leaning forward and pressing down if the pull-up bothers you.

One of the main things is to keep track of where you are all the way around. You will get so you can see more and more, the more you practice. Remember that almost anyone can take an airplane through a Loop—but a military pilot should be able to make a balanced pattern in a vertical plane and come out smack on the reference line.

Auxiliary Controls: In cruising positions, throttle changing.

## Procedure

1. Clear the area with exceptional care.
2. Choose a road, section line or fence line —for orientation.
3. From straight and level cruising flight, ease into a fairly steep dive parallel to your reference line and retard the throttle enough to keep from exceeding maximum rpm. When you reach a speed of approximately 165 mph, use considerable back pressure to start the airplane up on the arc of a circle and maintain the arc with steady pressure.
4. As the airplane starts upward, ease the throttle to the full advanced position for maximum power. Keep an eye on the reference line as long as you can see it.

5. Gradually relax the back pressure as speed decreases or you'll stall before you reach the inverted position at the top of the Loop.

6. As the airplane approaches the inverted position, throw your head back to pick up your reference line again and make corrections in attitude.

7. When the airplane is well started on the downward path, ease the throttle back well below cruising setting to avoid excessive loss of altitude, excessive rpm, and excessive speed.

8. As the airplane reaches the horizon and starts upward again, use full throttle and climb to gain altitude. When you slow down to cruising airspeed, resume level flight and adjust the throttle to cruising rpm.

### Suggestions

Smooth, positive back pressure is necessary to start the Loop but violent back stick causes too rapid loss of speed and may cause a stall near the top of the Loop. Judge the amount of back pressure necessary by the resistance of the stick.

If the nose of the airplane moved to the right of the intended flight path in the Loop, you probably either lowered the right wing during the pull-up (tendency to pull the stick toward the right shoulder), or used too much right rudder. If it moved to the left, there was probably insufficient correction for torque.

### Common Errors of Student

1. Does not clear the area.
2. Fails to use a reference point.
3. Starts maneuver at wrong airspeed.
4. Does not come straight back with stick.
5. Doesn't relax the stick properly when approaching top of the Loop.
6. Fails to correct for torque.
7. Doesn't adjust the throttle properly.
8. Doesn't throw head back to pick up the reference line.
9. Fails to make corrections in inverted position.
10. Dives too steeply.
11. Misses reference line because of poor orientation.
12. Doesn't regain lost altitude.

# SNAP ROLLS

Snap Rolls show you how a particular combination of control pressures will produce sudden "snaps" and how you can recover quickly.

The Snap Roll in Basic Training is a graceful, smoothly controlled maneuver. The entry calls for a smooth, positive buildup of pressure, rather than violent application of full stick and rudder. Likewise, the recovery requires a gradual relaxation of rudder pressure followed by gentle application of opposite rudder, rather than rough, full control movements.

Auxiliary Controls: In cruising positions.

### Procedure

1. Clear the area, establish a speed of 115 mph in the BT-13A (for the most satisfactory results), and raise the nose approximately 20° above the horizon in line with a reference point.

2. Build up positive back stick and rudder pressures simultaneously in the direction of the snap.

3. When these pressures reach a given point, the airplane will suddenly stall and enter the Snap Roll. Don't increase your back pressure after the stall occurs because you want to avoid a violent stall. The more complete the stall, the rougher the entry and the more difficult the recovery.

*Note:*

In entering a Snap Roll to the right, in the BT-13A, there is a tendency for the stick to jerk to the right. Resist this tendency, since the use of ailerons makes the snap more difficult to control.

4. When about one-half the way around, relax the rudder pressure used to enter the snap and smoothly apply opposite rudder. At approximately three-fourths of the way around, if the timing is correct, the rotation will begin to slow down. Then move the rudder smoothly toward the neutral position.

5. When wings roll out level, hold only sufficient rudder pressure to correct for torque. This is the most difficult part of the maneuver and requires good timing and considerable practice to stop wings in a level position with the nose on the reference point. Throughout the maneuver, hold the stick in approximately the same position fore and aft as when the stall occurred. With the stick in this position, you can recover with the nose of the airplane slightly above the horizon.

Slight variation in rigging causes airplanes of the same type to react differently in Snap Rolls and this requires changes in the use of controls.

Because of torque, more rudder is required to start a snap to the right than to the left and more rudder is required in recovering from a right snap than from a left snap.

### Common Errors of Student

1. Fails to look around before starting the maneuver.

2. Enters at wrong speed and holds the nose too high or too low.

3. Moves controls abruptly when entering or stopping the roll.

4. Uses ailerons before the snap occurs.

5. Uses rudder at the wrong time during recovery.

6. Holds too much rudder after recovery.

# SLOW ROLLS

This maneuver is accurately described by its name. It is a slow, complete rotation of the airplane around its longitudinal axis. It gives you practice in analyzing the use of controls in continuously changing and unfamiliar attitudes. Slow Rolls also show you how easy it is to fly upside down when you know how. Throughout most of a Slow Roll you are flying by the "pit of your stomach" instead of the "seat of your pants." You'll find this is great stuff when you get used to it.

Slow Rolls are a real test of your progress as a pilot. The man who can turn out consistently good Slow Rolls is getting there fast. Use every bit of skill you have and you will rapidly become more proficient.

Auxiliary Controls: In cruising positions.

### Procedure

1. Be sure the area is clear and select a small cloud or landmark on the horizon to be used as a reference point.

2. Dive the airplane enough to gain a speed of approximately 140 mph and smoothly apply full throttle as you raise the nose approximately 20° above the horizon in line with the reference point.

3. To execute a Slow Roll to the left, use left aileron and left rudder pressure to start the roll.

4. At approximately 45° through the roll, gradually shift from left to right rudder pressure to hold the nose on the point.

5. Use left aileron pressure throughout the maneuver to keep the airplane rolling. At the inverted position, the stick should be well forward and over to the left.

6. Shortly after passing the inverted position, relax right rudder and gradually increase left rudder together with forward stick to hold the nose on the point.

7. As the airplane passes the vertical bank position, gradually move the stick in an arc from forward and left toward a point slightly back of neutral. Time it so the stick reaches neutral just as the airplane rolls out in level flight with the nose on the horizon in line with the reference point.

8. Reduce the throttle to cruising when back in level flight.

9. You will notice as you recover that the airplane is in a slight skid and controls are slightly crossed. This is normal. Neutralize controls slowly so the airplane won't veer.

*Note:*

In Slow Rolls to the right use exactly opposite movements with extra rudder pressure to counteract torque. Satisfactory Slow Rolls in the Basic Trainer require movements of the controls through a large range. Students with short legs should use cushions and make necessary rudder pedal adjustments before take-off.

### Common Errors of Student

1. Fails to look around, to use a reference point, or to gain proper airspeed.

2. Fails to start with nose above the horizon.

3. Doesn't coordinate stick and rudder during roll-in.

4. Fails to use top rudder soon enough after starting roll.

5. Lets nose down when inverted because of insufficient forward stick.

6. Relaxes on aileron pressure, causing roll to slow up or stop. (This is a frequent error during the early part of Slow Roll practice.)

7. Allows the nose to "slice" out while wings are in the vertical position during last half of maneuver. (This is caused by relaxing the forward pressure on the stick and by insufficient top rudder. Even experienced pilots persistently make this mistake.)

8. Does not hold the point.

# SAFETY BELT

# FASTENED ?

# "Use Yourself as the Pivot Point!"

Think hard on this one because it will be a big help to you when you understand it. One of the easiest ways to orient yourself in Slow Rolls (and in other acrobatics) is to use yourself as the pivot point and to remember that control movements in relation to the pilot always remain the same regardless of the attitude of the airplane.

Try this out. Select a cloud or the end of a road on the distant horizon as a reference point. If the reference point is to your right, you will use right rudder to bring the nose back on the point. This is true when the airplane is in level flight, when the wings are vertical, when the airplane is inverted or in any other attitude.

Likewise remember that you can always bring the nose "toward yourself" by back stick pressure and move the nose "away from yourself" by using forward pressure. You can move the left wing "away from yourself" and bring the right wing "toward yourself" with left aileron, and vice versa. By thinking of the problem in this way, and through practice in relating directions to yourself, you can much more easily determine which controls to use when the airplane is in unusual attitudes.

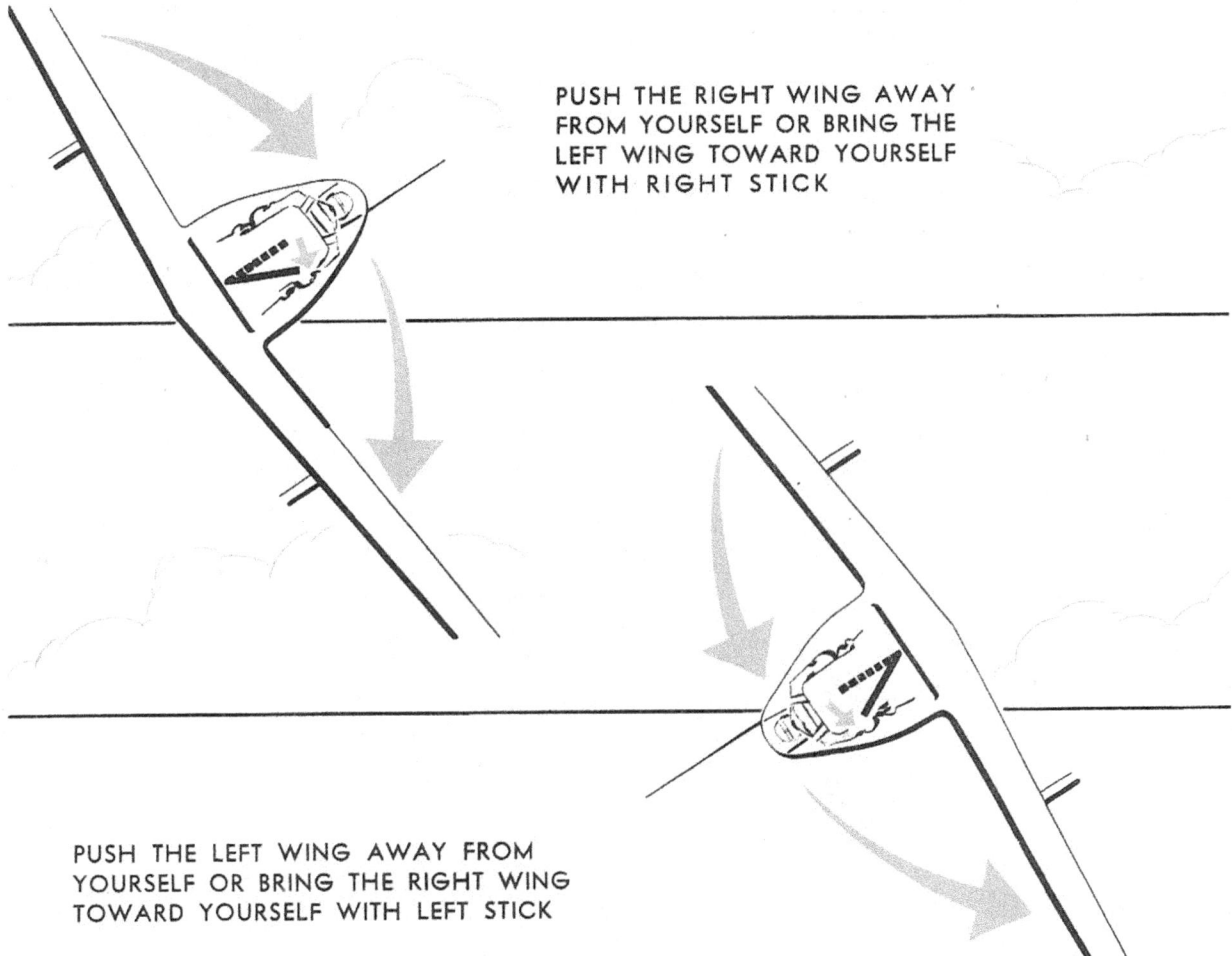

PUSH THE RIGHT WING AWAY FROM YOURSELF OR BRING THE LEFT WING TOWARD YOURSELF WITH RIGHT STICK

PUSH THE LEFT WING AWAY FROM YOURSELF OR BRING THE RIGHT WING TOWARD YOURSELF WITH LEFT STICK

103

PUSH THE NOSE AWAY FROM
YOURSELF WITH FORWARD STICK

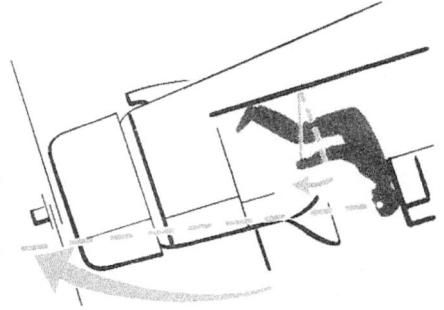

**REFERENCE
POINT**

BRING THE NOSE
TOWARD YOURSELF
WITH BACK STICK

MOVE THE NOSE TO YOUR
LEFT WITH LEFT RUDDER

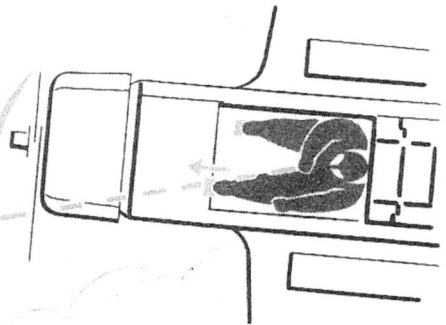

**REFERENCE
POINT**

MOVE THE NOSE
TO YOUR RIGHT WITH
RIGHT RUDDER

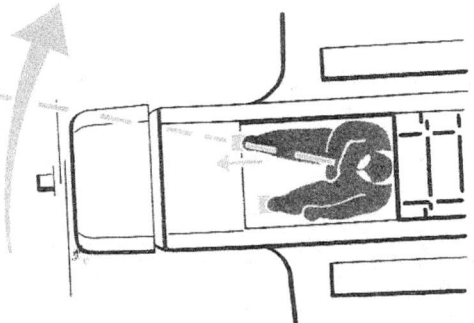

# HALF ROLL AND REVERSE

This is a difficult maneuver but it is well worth the time and attention of every pilot. Half Rolls teach you how to roll smoothly out of an inverted position back to straight and level flight. It is important for a pilot to know how to do this in case his airplane should be thrown into an upside-down position close to the ground.

This maneuver requires unusually good coordination, precision blending of controls, and careful judgment. The test of proficiency lies in not losing altitude below the lowest point of the entering dive.

Auxiliary Controls: In cruising positions.

## Procedure

1. Start the maneuver exactly as you would a slow roll, except you enter it at a speed of approximately 150 mph.
2. Slow roll the airplane onto its back; stop it there momentarily with the nose slightly above the reference point.
3. Then slow roll back to level flight in the direction opposite to the roll-in.

## Note:

This maneuver is preferred over the "diving" recovery from inverted flight because in a diving recovery the modern, "clean" airplane gains too much speed and loses too much altitude.

### Common Errors of Student

1. Holds the airplane on its back for too long a time.
2. Loses excessive altitude.
3. Stalls in the inverted position.

Other errors are the same as in Slow Rolls.

# THE IMMELMANN

An Immelmann is a composite maneuver combining the first half of a loop with the last half of a slow roll. Proper execution in the Basic Trainer requires excellent timing, good orientation, and precision coordination of controls from the moment you start the upward arc until you roll out in upright, level position at the top of the loop.

Consistently good Immelmanns require maximum performance of the airplane . . . one of the most important objectives of Basic Training. It takes good flying to do a good Immelmann in the Basic Trainer. When your Immelmanns are consistently smooth, you know you are beginning to master the technique of maximum performance.

Auxiliary Controls: In cruising positions, throttle changing.

## Procedure

1. Clear the area thoroughly, line up on a straight road, section line, or other suitable reference line, and ease into a fairly steep dive. As you increase speed, retard throttle so as not to exceed maximum engine rpm.
2. At approximately 180 to 185 mph apply definite back pressure to start the airplane up on the arc of a loop. As the climb begins, smoothly apply full throttle.
3. As speed decreases, relax back pressure on the stick, or the airplane may stall before reaching the top of the loop.

4. As you near the inverted position throw back your head to observe the horizon and to hold a straight flight path.

5. Just as the nose reaches a point approximately 20° above the horizon, execute the last half of a slow roll.

6. For example, to start the roll to the left, apply strong left aileron pressure and simultaneously use a slight amount of right rudder. Then relax right rudder and apply left rudder to hold the nose on the point. Maintain left aileron pressure throughout to keep the airplane rolling.

7. Use exactly opposite controls in the roll-out to the right except that you will need much more opposite rudder at the start of the roll.

8. Check your position against the reference line as soon as you complete the maneuver. Properly executed, this roll will bring the airplane back to straight and level flight with 180° of change in heading.

9. As you regain cruising speed, retard the throttle to cruising setting.

## Common Errors of Student

1. Fails to clear the area properly.
2. Uses insufficient airspeed.
3. Uses insufficient pull-up at the start of the loop with too large a pattern, and stalls.
4. Fails to relax back pressure as speed decreases.
5. Begins roll with nose too far above or too far below the horizon.
6. Snaps airplane at the top of loop instead of slow rolling out.
7. Uses insufficient aileron pressure and (or) excessive top rudder.
8. Moves controls erratically during recovery.
9. Loses track of flight path . . . poor orientation.
10. Doesn't roll out properly. (Review and practice of slow rolls may be necessary.)

*Formation Flying*

The secret of perfect formation flying is perfect teamwork . . . a leader who knows how to lead, and wingmen who know how to follow every move their leader makes.

In good formation work the three airplanes will function almost like one big airplane, banking together, climbing together, turning together, with wingmen as responsive to every move of the leader as his own airplane is. That's the way it is in combat. Three P-51's have the eyes, the manpower, and the **firepower** of an airplane three times as big as any one of them. That's the secret of their fighting power.

Your first objective is to learn how to hold your position in a 3-airplane element. You have to know how to fly together to be able to fight together. Work every minute to perfect your skill. It is important to safety and to your ultimate success in combat.

## VISUAL SIGNALS
## FOR FORMATION FLYING

Experienced pilots don't need signals to fly formation. They simply follow the leader. However, you will find signals extremely helpful in telling you what comes next. Here are the standardized signals used in Basic Schools:

107

SIGNAL: Rocking the ailerons before take-off
(Repeated by wingmen to show readiness)
MEANING: Get ready for take-off

SIGNAL: A series of very slight dives and zooms
MEANING: We're going to land

SIGNAL: Moving fist back and forth
MEANING: Change your propeller

SIGNAL: Rotating fist as if turning crank
in clockwise direction
MEANING: Flaps up

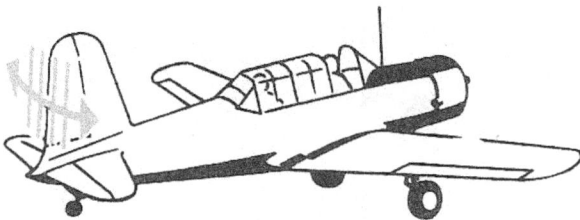

SIGNAL: Fishtailing the airplane
MEANING: Open interval

SIGNAL: In counter-clockwise direction
MEANING: Flaps down. (If necessary, hold up five
fingers for five turns of crank, etc.)

SIGNAL: Rocking the wings slightly
MEANING: Close interval

SIGNAL: Turning fist with thumb extended
MEANING: Change gas tanks (if necessary)

SIGNAL: Pointing with forearm and finger or thumb
to right or left
MEANING: Turn to right or left

SIGNAL: Holding hand to headset and then swinging
up and down in front of face, as in "cease firing"
MEANING: Radio out of commission

108

# FOLLOW THE LEADER

Success in formation flying depends a great deal upon the interest, enthusiasm, and mutual confidence of the leader and his wingmen. Wingmen must have absolute confidence in their leader and the leader must be able to rely on his wingmen or the formation will be flown raggedly.

The leader is your Safety Pilot. He will plan ahead and allow plenty of room for maneuvers. He has to spot other airplanes, keep the formation clear of other traffic, and never fly too close to obstacles. The leader will usually fly at slightly reduced throttle because a wingman can't catch up unless he has a margin of power to use. A good leader will insist on precision flying and second-by-second teamwork. That is the only way he can develop a competent team.

Apply yourself, follow the leader smoothly and promptly, and try to anticipate the next move before it happens. Remember that skill in formation flying is of every-day practical use in combat flying.

## Taxiing

1. Normally you will taxi in Vee formation but the leader will direct you to taxi in echelon when necessary. Echelon away from obstacles.

2. Swing right and left with the leader as he clears the path ahead.

3. The leader will make wide, **gradual** turns. Otherwise he would pull across in front of one wingman and far ahead of the other one. The inside airplane should drop back slightly and head in toward the leader's tail. The outside airplane travels farther than the others and should increase throttle slightly.

*Positions in Formation*

HORIZONTAL SEPARATION

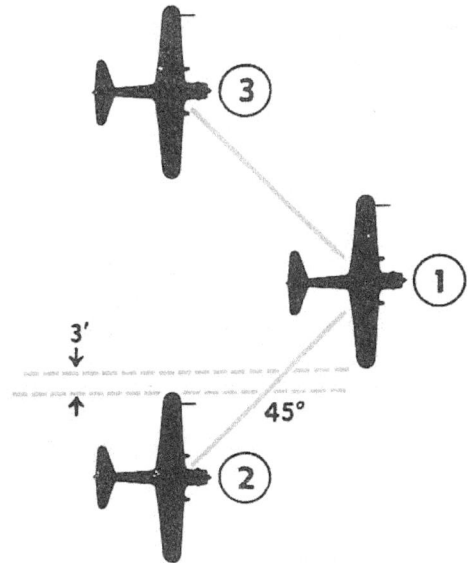

VERTICAL SEPARATION

# TURNS IN FORMATION

OUTSIDE WINGMAN HAS
GREATER DISTANCE TO
TRAVEL...SPEEDS UP ➡

⬅ INSIDE WINGMAN HAS
SHORTER DISTANCE TO
TRAVEL...SLOWS DOWN

*Always Watch the Leader*

4. Watch the leader and do as he does. Remember that you move together as one big airplane.

### Take-Off

1. Watch the leader. He is the look-out and gives the signal for taking off.

2. Take off in Vee formation. The leader will use slightly reduced throttle so that the wingmen will have extra power if they need it.

3. Use your throttle properly on take-off or you'll go shooting by the leader. Remember that you don't need full throttle on take-off. Stay well out to the side to avoid the prop wash of the lead airplane.

### Turns

1. Again the leader will do most of the looking around.

2. Anticipate what is coming. Get so you can read your leader's mind. Timing is all-important.

3. Bank and turn with the leader. Inside airplane will drop down and retard the throttle slightly. Outside man will bank up and add enough throttle to hold his position—wings of all three airplanes should be in the same plane.

### Landings

1. The leader will watch out for traffic. Normally he will use a long 45° approach, will make the whole traffic pattern wider and will set the downwind and base leg farther out. Keep the pattern in mind so you will know what to expect.

2. The formation will use a power-on approach and fly traffic at about 110 mph. The leader will make the last turn at about 100 mph because the inside wingman will be slower and must be able to maintain speed safely above a stall.

3. Use slightly more flaps than the leader. Then you will be able to stay behind. More throttle will bring you forward but it's hard to fall back.

4. The glide will be somewhat faster than normal, and wingmen should move out and drop slightly lower down than the leader. The leader will keep you well above all obstacles.

5. Go easy on the brakes. The leader will usually add a little throttle after he is on the ground to keep you from overshooting him.

### General Rules for Wingmen

1. Keep your eyes on the leader and bank with him, turn with him, stick with him.

2. Maintain distance sideways from leader by using rudder only for small corrections and rudder and ailerons for greater corrections.

3. **Anticipate throttle adjustments.** If you give full throttle to catch up, don't leave it on until you are back in position or you'll go shooting by the leader. Before the leader starts to turn, increase your throttle if you are on the outside of the turn, decrease throttle if you are on the inside of the turn. Take into consideration the lag in acceleration and the effects of momentum.

4. Keep making small corrections constantly to hold the right position. It's a lot easier to make several slight adjustments than to regain your position after definitely falling behind or veering to one side.

5. The important thing is steady **accurate flying** rather than **too close** a formation.

### Common Errors of Student

1. Gets out of position, drops below lead plane. (Or gets too far out, gets too close, gets behind.)

2. Uses too much throttle adjustment.

3. Flies in position with one wing down.

4. Corrects too much with dangerous results.

5. Doesn't watch the lead plane closely enough.

6. Can't keep his head out of the cockpit when adjusting auxiliary controls.

7. Can't change position properly.

8. Doesn't know signals (or change of position signals).

9. Doesn't drop down on inside of turn or take high position on outside of turn. Drops out on turns.

10. Taxies too close in formation or too far out. Jams on brakes too hard. Can't control airplane.

11. Reacts too slowly.

12. Lands too close in, too far out, too far behind, or over-runs lead plane.

# Vision at Night

Vision at night differs from vision in the daytime because you use different parts of the eye. You use a relatively small bull's eye area of the retina at the back of the eye for most of your day vision. This area is filled with tiny organs called cones which enable you to make out color and fine detail by looking directly at an object in bright light. But you also see objects to one side with the outer area of the retina which contains few cones but many rods.

These rods will not register color or detail but do register movements of objects and picture them in different shades of gray.

The bull's eye area is the most efficient part of the eye for day vision but is 1,000 times less sensitive in dim light than the rods in the outer area of the retina. Thus in bright or normal light one part of your eye is doing most of the work and in dim light, another part of the eye does most of your seeing.

## Night Blind Spot

Since the bull's eye part of your eye is inefficient in dim light, you have what amounts to a blind spot of 5° to 10° in the center of your vision when you look directly at a point or object at night. That's why you can see a thing much more clearly by looking slightly to one side of it. The best way is to pass your eyes slowly back and forth across the points or areas you are observing. It's easier to move your head slowly than to move your eyes. Don't concentrate on any one thing. Look out both sides of the cockpit, keep your vision shifting, and view objects off center.

## TO SEE THE TARGET MOST CLEARLY AT NIGHT, DON'T LOOK DIRECTLY AT IT

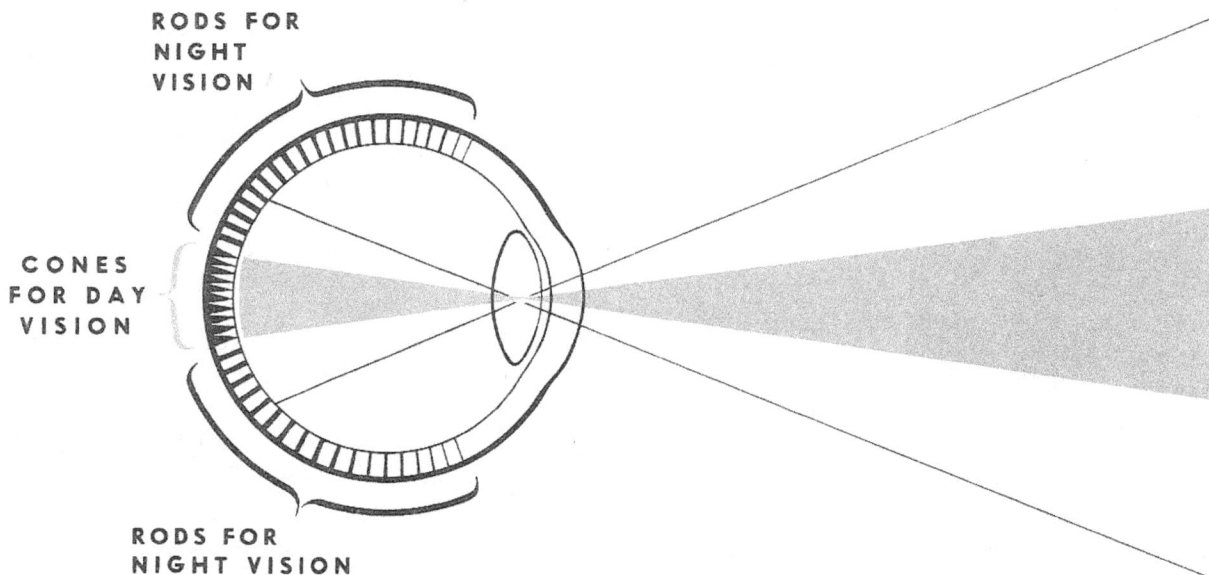

RODS FOR NIGHT VISION

CONES FOR DAY VISION

RODS FOR NIGHT VISION

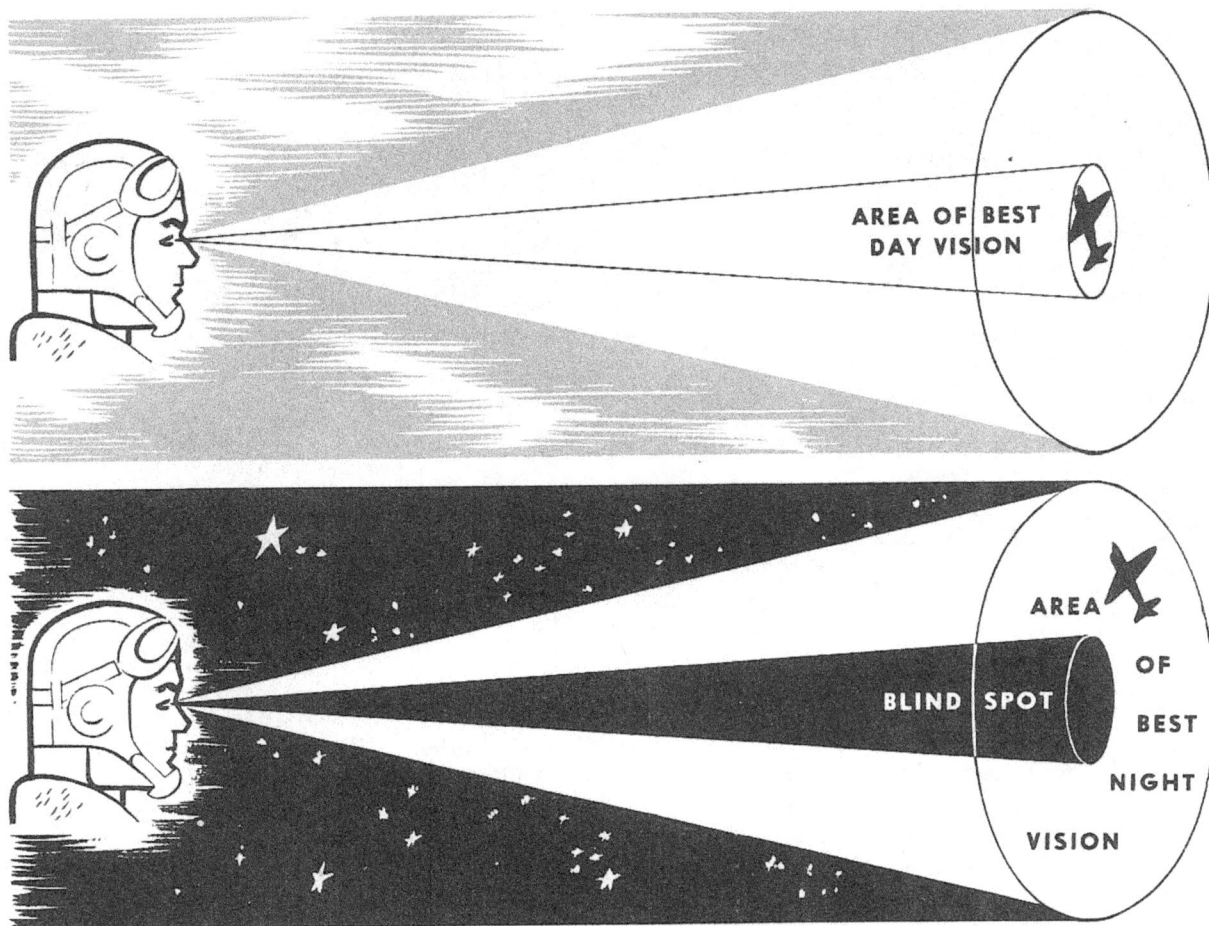

AREA OF BEST DAY VISION

AREA OF BEST NIGHT VISION

BLIND SPOT

## Practice

Since different parts of your eyes are on duty at night, good day vision doesn't necessarily mean you can see well at night. Those with the best night vision can see with only one-tenth of the light needed by those with the poorest night vision. The average person has never trained the night-seeing parts of his eyes and practice will make a surprising difference. You will find you can greatly improve your night vision by practicing off-center glances at objects in dim light out-of-doors at night. Through such practice some men have doubled the power of their night vision. Here are several tips that will help you see better at night:

1. Adapt your eyes to darknes. Stay in a dark room or sit outside in the dark watching night flying for 30 minutes before take-off. Don't expose your eyes to any bright light inside or outside the hangar or the aircraft.

2. Keep all lights in the aircraft turned as low as possible, and when taxiing by flood-lights or when spotted in a searchlight, look the other way.

3. Read instruments, maps, etc., rapidly and then look away. Better still, use one eye. The other eye will see in the dark independently.

4. Eat food rich in Vitamin A—eggs, butter, cheese, liver, apricots, peaches, carrots, squash, peas, and especially cod liver oil and all types of greens.

5. Remember that flight at altitudes above 5,000 ft. without oxygen seriously affects night vision. At 12,000 ft. without oxygen, night vision is only one-half as efficient.

6. Keep windows and goggles scrupulously clean and free from scratches. Dirt and scratches distort vision and cause deceptive reflections. Fly with the canopy open most of the time, especially on take-offs, landings, and in traffic.

# NIGHT FLYING

Night flying is not difficult but it is different—and the differences are extremely important. You will be many times repaid for hard work on the ground learning radio procedure, the location of zones, and any tips the Flight Commander or your instructor may give you.

The purpose of local night flying is to teach you how to land using various types of lighting, how to fly in the dark, and how to orient yourself at night. Remember that night cross-countries will be started soon and everything you learn now will help you then.

### Ask Questions

Make sure you understand everything you are told about zones, traffic, signals, etc. Night time is no time for confusion. Ask questions and keep asking them until you have a clear mental picture of what is expected.

### Dual Instruction

Dual instruction will be brief. Usually your instructor will make the first take-off and landing and then ask you to take over. After three or four landings you'll probably be soloing. Keep on your toes, learn all you can during the dual flight, and make a mental note of anything you don't understand. Following are practical tips that will help you turn in a better performance and help you avoid common errors. Ask your instructor for further explanations of any points which aren't clear.

1. Know your radio and know the proper procedure for sending and acknowledging messages. Failure in radio communication destroys control and multiplies hazards.

2. Be brief and direct when transmitting and don't try to use the microphone during taxiing, landing, or take-offs when the airplane needs all your attention.

3. Radio failure usually comes from faulty operation. Check the Hi-Lo switch, the volume, the tuning dial, the interphone switch, and headset plug-in. When your radio fails completely in flight, blink your landing lights to notify the tower, and watch for biscuit-gun light signals from the tower.

### Before Take-Off

1. Know the system of signal lights, traffic, and zones.

2. Know the location of all switches.

3. At the time specified, make cockpit check, start the engine, turn on the Navigation and Passing lights, and check the engine. **Keep Cockpit Lights Low.**

4. Set altimeter carefully. A faulty altimeter reading is especially dangerous at night.

5. Be sure the radio is working; tune it carefully and LOUD. It will fade during take-off and traffic flying. Check in with radio con-

trol when ready, and promptly follow instructions for taxiing and take-off.

### Take-Off

1. Keep the canopy open. This eliminates confusing reflections. Note the hangar line and other reference points.

2. Take off (when cleared) toward a boundary light or some definite reference point. Hold 'er right on that point.

3. The sparks and flames shooting out of the exhaust do not mean the airplane is on fire. The same thing happens in the day time but you don't see it.

4. You will plunge into sudden darkness soon after take-off (especially out of a floodlight). Don't let this confuse you. Hold your flight path and accustom your eyes to the darkness.

5. Don't look back at the lights of the field. Orient yourself ahead and to the side. Check your instruments with a **quick** glance and don't let the seat of your pants fool you.

6. It's just like a daytime take-off, but keep your turns much more shallow, stick closely to the traffic pattern, and obey instructions to the letter.

7. Don't be in a hurry to close your canopy —keep it open until you reach your zone. If reflections blind you when you close it, open it again and check your cockpit lights. One may be pointing up and causing confusing reflections.

THE LAW: If your engine should fail on take-off, there is only one thing to do— LAND STRAIGHT AHEAD (or at a very slight angle to avoid obstructions). Did you read that? LAND STRAIGHT AHEAD. Now read it again and **believe it.** Don't try to turn back **EVER.**

### During Flight

1. Keep radio loud and watch for signals.

2. If assigned, go to your zone and altitude immediately.

3. Fly the zone as instructed. Don't wander out of it. There are other airplanes in the sky flown by students who are also just learning night flying. Maybe their night vision isn't too good.

4. Remember, this is the same airplane you fly in the daytime and the same sky. You have the same fuel problem, the same controls to use, and you need room in which to maneuver. Don't let the instrument board hypnotize you. Keep looking around, keep oriented, and keep referring to your zone and traffic check points. Lights in the distance can be deceiving if you stare at them steadily.

### Landings

1. Leave your position or zone in the prescribed manner and come in immediately when called.

2. Don't forget to watch for, acknowledge, and immediately obey landing signals.

3. Watch out for traffic, don't get too close to other airplanes, keep the canopy open, and don't be fooled by reflections.

4. Use your regular 90° side approach; enter the base leg as prescribed and cut the throttle at the key point on the base leg as in a daylight landing.

5. Establish a glide that is 5 to 10 mph faster than in the daytime.

6. Complete the last turn at 500 ft. or more. Don't get into a dangerously low turn (or cross controls) trying to line up for landing.

7. After that, it's like daytime landings. Use necessary flaps and, if undershooting, use your throttle **at once.**

8. Break the glide lower than in the daytime and hold the airplane dead ahead on its roll toward a boundary light.

9. Avoid a tendency to ground-loop because of the confusion of lights. Look out both sides of the cockpit and don't focus and hold your eyes on one spot.

10. Don't waste time. Clear the landing strip immediately and, if signalled to go to the line, go in quickly.

11. Throughout the landing, be alert for radio instructions and, if in doubt, **go around again.**

### Floodlight Landings

1. Shoot to land in the first third of the floodlights.

2. Don't try to land on top of the beam of light . . . a common error.

3. There is always a temptation to level off too high when there is dust or moisture in the air. It is much safer to come in faster and land slightly wheels-first.

### Winglight Landings

During the second phase of night flying you will usually make a few floodlight landings, several landings using both floodlights and winglights, and as many winglight landings as possible. Remember these things about winglight landings:

1. Turn both winglights on after completing the roll-out from the last turn, **not before.** Make the turn high enough to allow time for your eyes to become adjusted to the light.

**DON'T SIGHT DOWN THE WINGLIGHT BEAM**

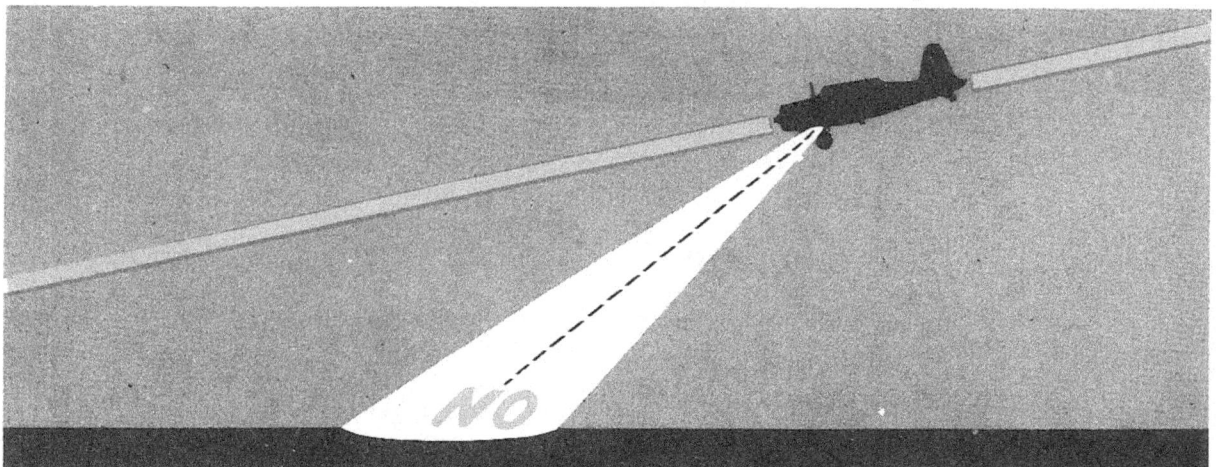

2. Don't look down the beam of light. Stay relaxed and keep oriented by looking around at the airdrome lights and at surrounding objects.

3. Use a normal degree of flaps in the Vultee Trainer. If you use no flaps, the airplane tends toward a nose-high attitude and your winglights may shine too high to illuminate the ground. Excessive flaps steepen the gliding angle. This will bring the ground suddenly into view and may cause you to jerk back on the stick too quickly.

4. Level off when your lights pick up **detail** of grass, weeds, etc. Slowly and steadily move the stick back. Don't wait too long, and then jerk it back. The tendency is to level off too low when using winglights and too high in floodlights.

5. Turn off winglights as soon as convenient after the airplane is on the ground.

### Landings on Lighted Runways

If the schedule permits, you will be given practice in landing on lighted runways. You will probably use both winglights and runway lights on the first two or three landings and then use the runway lights only.

Use a regular 90° side approach but maintain a glide 5 to 10 mph faster than in the daytime. The runway lights make it easy to determine your height above the ground, to judge how you are coming in, and to hold the airplane straight during the landing roll. This is the easiest type of night landing and should give you no trouble if you keep alert.

### Emergency Landings

This is the most commonly used procedure for emergency night landing. Check it against the procedure at your school.

1. If possible, notify the tower by radio of the emergency and that you are coming in.

2. If your radio won't work, blink your landing lights at the tower until the biscuit-gun signals you what to do.

3. If neither your lights nor radio work, get out of your zone, approach the field well outside the traffic pattern and fly right over the tower at about 100 feet. When you get the green light, enter the traffic pattern and come on in. Keep watch for further light signals.

4. In extreme emergency do everything possible to call attention to your predicament and come on in, avoiding traffic as best you can.

### Common Errors of Student

1. Uses poor radio procedure. Doesn't acknowledge (or obey) instructions.

2. Circles too far out of zone.

3. Lands too close to other airplanes.

4. Overshoots or undershoots.

5. Flies with his head in the cockpit.

6. Sets base leg too far out (or too close in).

7. Flies erratically in climbs and glides.

8. Uses improper taxiing technique.

9. Doesn't look around enough.

10. Forgets the cockpit procedure. (Flaps, throttle, propeller control, etc.)

11. Gets stick back too soon (or not soon enough).

12. Nervous, doesn't settle down.

13. Doesn't use right amount of flaps. Is slow or forgets to adjust flaps, propeller control, stabilizer, etc.

14. Overcontrols in attempting to hold position.

15. Fails to anticipate throttle adjustments.

16. Doesn't adapt eyes to darkness before take-off.

17. Turns cockpit lights up too high.

18. Doesn't practice night vision.

# Navigation Flights

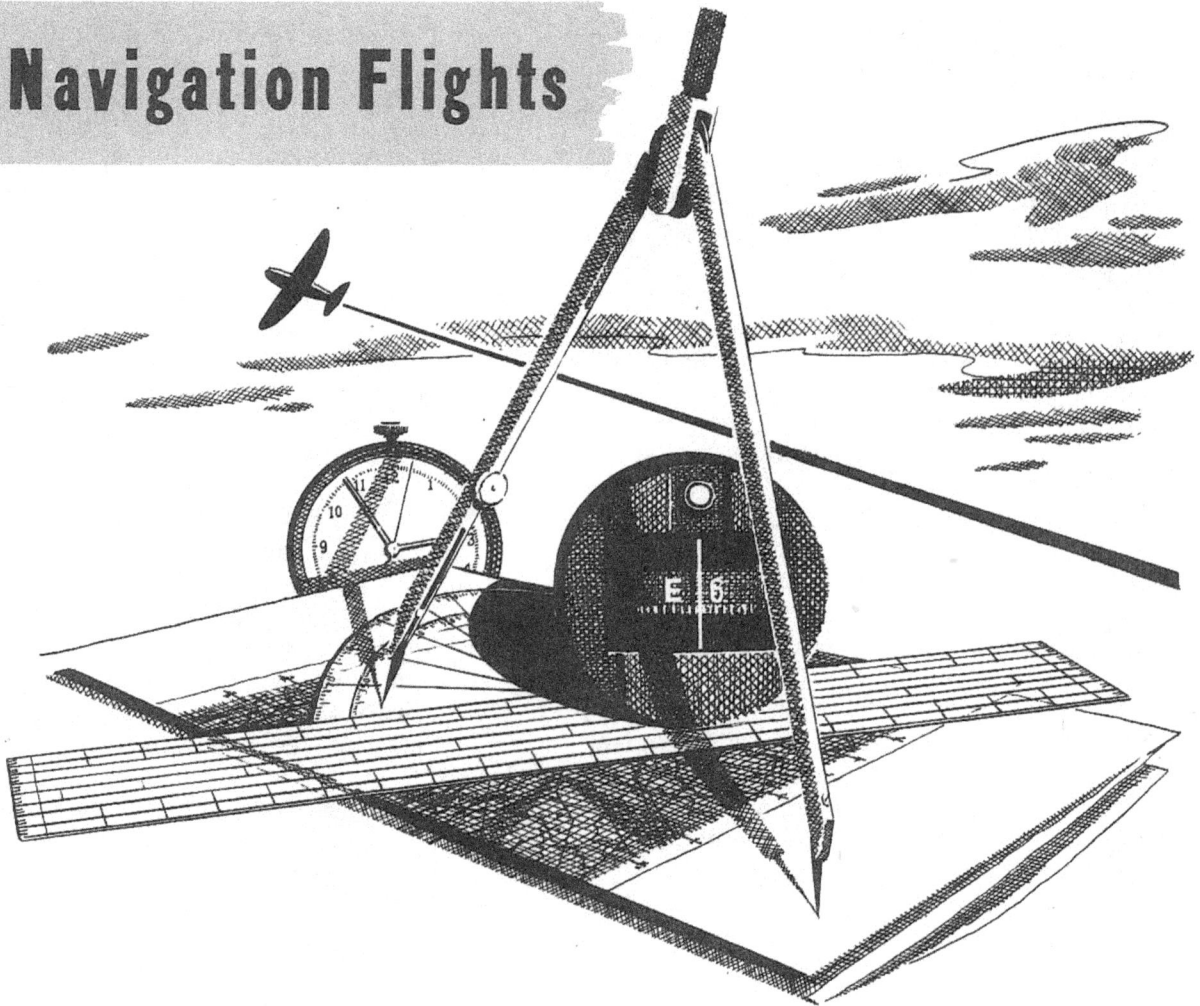

One of the main objectives in flying airplanes is to get from one place to another quickly. Since there are no regular highway signs in the sky, a pilot must know at least the fundamentals of navigation; otherwise he will get lost and feel very uncomfortable and foolish about it. In combat, the ability of a pilot to navigate becomes a matter of life and death. Fighter aircraft are constantly increasing their range of action. A bomber pilot whose navigator is incapacitated must know how to find his way home, or his plane and crew may be forced down in enemy territory.

You don't have to learn everything about navigation at this stage of training. But it is worth while to learn everything given here and learn it well. To be sure your first cross country is a success, you must know how to figure the correct headings, how to plot your course on the map, how to read the map and identify check points, and what to do in an emergency.

## Map Reading

Remember that there are two kinds of maps issued by operations offices, Sectional Maps and Regional Maps. A Sectional Map uses a scale of 1 to 500,000 and a Regional Map uses a scale of 1 to 1,000,000. In other words, a lake on a Sectional Map will look twice as large as it will on a Regional Map. Regional Maps don't show roads and many other details. Tuck this fact away in your memory for the day when you inadvertently pick up a Regional Map and wonder why you can't find things on it.

You will be using a Sectional Map on your

cross country flights in Basis Training. Get one for your area at the first opportunity and learn every symbol by heart so that when you are flying along and spot one on the map, it will shout its name at you. You don't have time in the air to refer to the explanatory legend to find out what a symbol means.

Listen to every word your flying instructor and navigation instructor have to say about map reading and get in a lot of good hard looking at your map before you go on your one-hour map reading flight with your instructor. With proper preparation, you'll see three times as much of what he shows you and be that much more certain of good pilotage on your first cross country.

## Tips on Identifying Check Points

1. Transmission lines are sometimes hard to see from the air in open country but you can easily see the swath cut for them through wooded country.

2. Remember that all small towns or villages are represented on the map by small circles of the same size whether the town is merely a gas station along the road or comprises a number of buildings. Only towns shown in yellow are reliable check points.

3. Near larger towns on the map, look for little notices of underpasses, tall buildings, water towers, etc. These help you to be sure of the identity of the town. Look for roads leading in and out of the town in relation to your compass heading.

4. Intersections of roads and railroads in relation to a town give you a good check point. Check the twists, turns, and angles at which they intercept one another.

5. Oil derricks and storage tanks are easily recognizable from the air. Check to make sure that the airport, race track, or other feature is on the right side of a town.

6. Remember, when flying in the mountains, that lookout towers and ranger stations are almost always prominently placed on a peak or a high ridge and are often silhouetted against the sky.

7. Many dirt roads don't show on the map. You will quickly learn to distinguish the clean, gray ribbon of a paved road from a dirt road. Don't let wishful thinking cause you to identify a road incorrectly. Check the twists and turns in the road, the angle at which it intercepts a railroad, and the side on which you find a railroad or river. This will tell you whether you have found the right or wrong road on the map. Remember

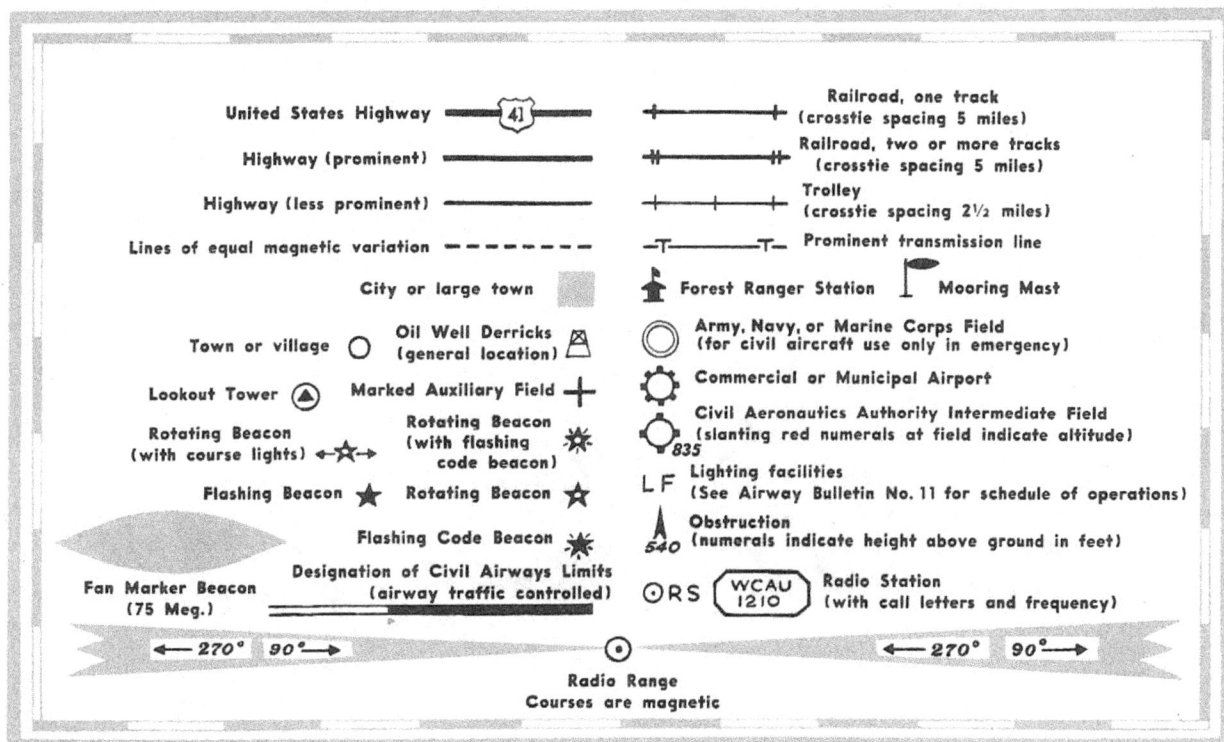

United States Highway

Highway (prominent)

Highway (less prominent)

Lines of equal magnetic variation

City or large town

Town or village

Oil Well Derricks (general location)

Lookout Tower

Marked Auxiliary Field

Rotating Beacon (with course lights)

Rotating Beacon (with flashing code beacon)

Flashing Beacon

Rotating Beacon

Flashing Code Beacon

Fan Marker Beacon (75 Meg.)

Designation of Civil Airways Limits (airway traffic controlled)

Railroad, one track (crosstie spacing 5 miles)

Railroad, two or more tracks (crosstie spacing 5 miles)

Trolley (crosstie spacing 2½ miles)

Prominent transmission line

Forest Ranger Station     Mooring Mast

Army, Navy, or Marine Corps Field (for civil aircraft use only in emergency)

Commercial or Municipal Airport

Civil Aeronautics Authority Intermediate Field (slanting red numerals at field indicate altitude) 835

Lighting facilities LF (See Airway Bulletin No. 11 for schedule of operations)

Obstruction 540 (numerals indicate height above ground in feet)

Radio Station ORS WCAU 1210 (with call letters and frequency)

←270° 90°→        ←270° 90°→

Radio Range
Courses are magnetic

Lock

Silver W T

RR under

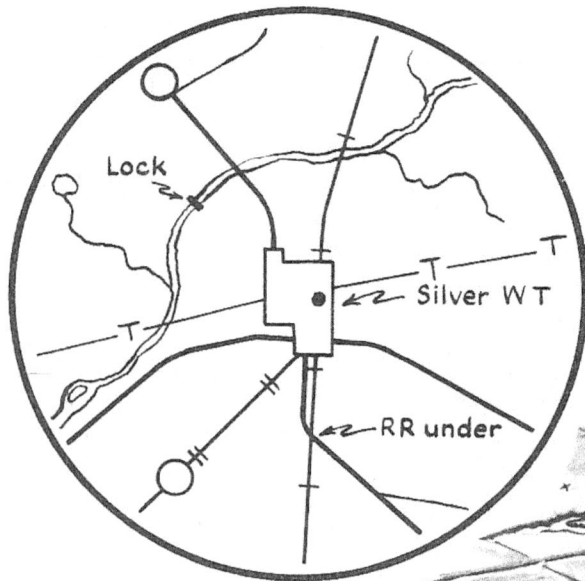

IS THAT THE TOWN?

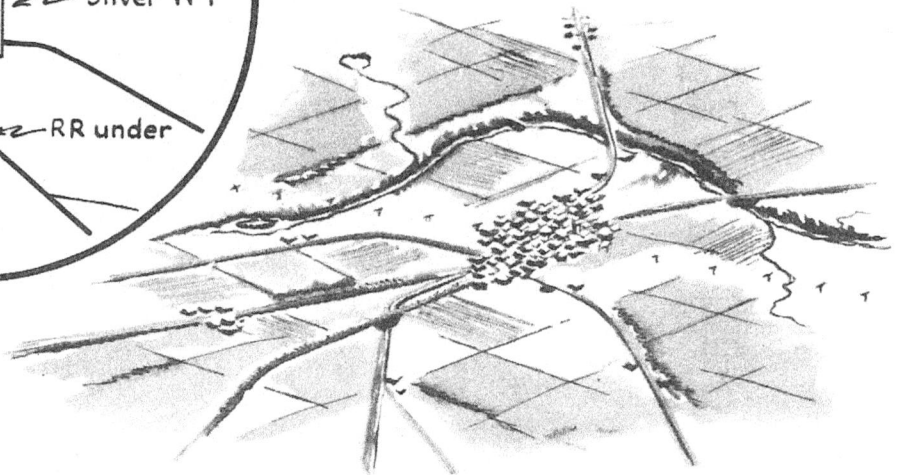

that new, paved roads may not be shown on your map.

8. Your map may show a body of water that you can't find on the ground. It may have dried up. Then you can usually see the dry lake or river bed from the air. At other seasons, whole areas of land may be covered with water that is not shown in your map. Keep in mind whether it is a rainy or dry season and, if necessary, rely on other check points such as roads, towns, railroads, etc.

9. You can use rivers in many ways. If there is no definite pattern of twists, look for bridges crossing the river, railroads and roads crossing or running parallel to it, towns near the river, etc. Be sure a town is on the same side of the river as shown on the map. In your eagerness to identify a town, don't be tempted to make a snap judgment. Think through every check point.

10. In some areas check points are hard to find. Then the contour of the ground may help you. The height of the terrain is shown in colors and marked clearly in figures. You know your altitude and can estimate your distance from the ground. This will tell you the general elevation of the ground over

YIPE

Caution: **KEEP THE CANOPY CLOSED WHEN HANDLING YOUR MAPS**

120

which you are flying. Isolated hills, mountains, or knolls are prominently shown on the map and easily seen from the air.

11. In mountainous country you can estimate the heights of outstanding peaks. Lakes in relation to mountains make excellent check points. It is often helpful to view a mountain range from a distance in relation to a specific check point. Ridges and marked erosions running from a mountain range into valleys make good check points.

12. Danger areas are outlined on the map but not on the ground. You have to use available check points to be sure to avoid these areas. Check Radio Facility Charts for up-to-date information.

13. If you suddenly have the feeling, "the map is not right," look for its publication date. If it is an old map, dams may have been built, large bodies of water backed up, and distinguishing characteristics of towns altered. But, don't blame your own mistakes on the map.

14. Most important of all—use your head! Look for every check point and check one against another. If several features agree then you know you're right. An incorrectly identified check point is worse than none at all. Note minor check points as you go along. They will lead you to more important ones.

# Your First Cross Country

Here are several suggestions that will help to make your first cross country a success:

1. Prepare your maps and figure headings carefully. Study every detail of the route on the map and try to visualize what your check points will look like..

2. Learn the air traffic rules applicable to your flight. See the Pilots' Information File.

3. Don't be a sap and risk unnecessary low flying, "buzzing," or other horseplay unless you want to get bounced out of the Air Forces. Violations are punished by elimination or trial in a military court.

4. Investigate your Cross Country Envelope and learn the use of each item.

5. Learn just as much as possible on the ground and it will help you to learn that much faster in the air.

### Checklist of Pilotage Terms

**True Course**=Straight line from departure to destination.

**True Heading**=True Course + or — correction for wind drift.

**Magnetic Heading**=True Heading corrected for magnetic variation (variation).

**Compass Heading**=Magnetic Heading corrected for compass error (deviation).

### By Guess and By Gosh!

Don't become a "by guess" and "by gosh" pilot. In ground school you learn to use the Weems plotter and your D-4 Computer. Master these navigation tools while you have the chance. In class, learn to figure your headings exactly because exact headings become tremendously important later when you are making long night cross country flights or flying through weather. But, at the same time, remember that you can't do a lot of paper work in the air. Learn the quick mental shortcuts for arriving at an approximate heading.

### Double Check Your Heading

Always, double-check your heading against common sense. Imagine that a hugh Compass Rose covers the area you are flying. Straight up on the map is North, 0° and 360°; at a right angle to the right is East, 90°; straight down is South, 180°; at right angles to the left is West, 270°. If you get this mental picture in your mind, you won't ever make the mistake of reading a heading of 270° when you are going from West to East. Common sense will tell you that an East heading will be somewhere near 90°; it can't possibly be 260°, 270°, or 280°. Know the relationship of directions on the map to the points of the compass.

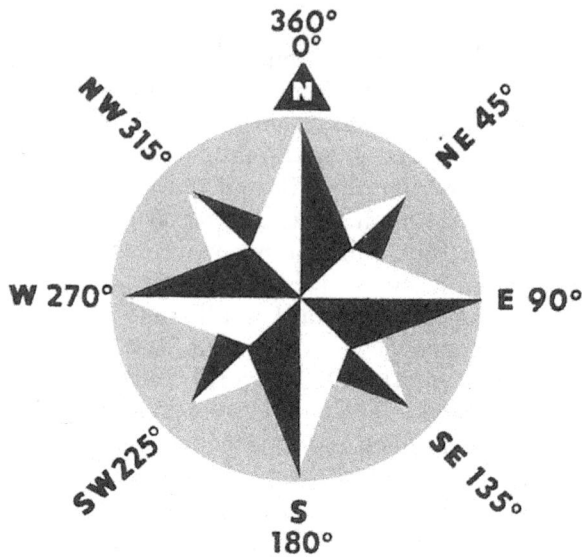

**360°**
**0°**
**N**
**NW 315°**
**NE 45°**
**W 270°**
**E 90°**
**SW 225°**
**SE 135°**
**S**
**180°**

ation is accurate except for wind drift. If you fly the heading and watch your check points carefully, you can see which way the wind is drifting and you can make the necessary drift correction. Then you won't go far wrong.

### Compass Heading

Your magnetic heading would be your compass heading except that there are certain deviations in each individual compass due to the magnetic influences set up by the radio, metal parts of the plane, etc. These deviations are shown on the Compass Correction Card in each airplane.

Thus, reading the right-hand column of the card shown here, the pilot wishing to fly a magnetic heading of 45° would fly a compass heading at 48°. A magnetic heading of 200° would call for a correction between "minus one" for 180° and "plus three" for 225° or approximately "plus one." Thus the magnetic heading of 200° would become a compass heading of 201°. A correction like this example is too small to bother with but corrections of four or five degrees are worth making. Normally you can ignore the figures in the left hand column on the card.

### Indicated Airspeed and True Airspeed

Close to the ground your True Airspeed and Indicated Airspeed will be approximately the same. As altitude increases and tempera-

### Short Cut

In emergency, if winds have changed, you can get your approximate heading by simply taking the heading from departure to destination and correcting for magnetic variation and deviation (compass error).

When applying magnetic variation remember:

"East is Least
and West is Best,"

meaning that you subtract East variation and add West variation.

A heading corrected for variation and devi-

COMPASS TO MAGNETIC

IF COMPASS HEADING IS 135 DEGREES, THE MAGNETIC HEADING IS 137 DEGREES

| Aircraft Comp. | | Date |
|---|---|---|
| **C** to **M** | | **M** to **C** |
| +1½ | . . . 000 . . . | —1½ |
| —3 | . . . 045 . . . | +3 |
| +1 | . . . 090 . . . | —1 |
| +2 | . . . 135 . . . | —2 |
| +1 | . . . 180 . . . | —1 |
| —3 | . . . 225 . . . | +3 |
| —1 | . . . 270 . . . | +1 |
| +1 | . . . 315 . . . | —1 |

MAGNETIC TO COMPASS

IF MAGNETIC HEADING IS 135 DEGREES, THE COMPASS HEADING IS 133 DEGREES

COMPASS CORRECTION CARD (T.O. No. 05-15-3)

ture goes down, your True Airspeed will be greater than that indicated. This is best shown by the following table:

| Altitude | Indicated Airspeed | Increase Indicated Airspeed to get Approximate True Airspeed as follows: | Approximate True Airspeed |
|---|---|---|---|
| 1,000 | 130 | ........ | 130 |
| 5,000 | 130 | 5% | 137 |
| 7,500 | 130 | 10% | 143 |
| 10,000 | 130 | 15% | 150 |
| 15,000 | 130 | 25% | 163 |

This is not an important consideration in your flights because you normally cruise at relatively low altitudes for short distances but later, when you are making long flights at higher altitudes, the difference between indicated and true airspeed is substantial.

## Marking Your Map

Mark your map as follows:

1. Draw a straight line to represent each leg of your flight.

2. Mark the magnetic heading for each leg. You won't know the compass correction until you get in the airplane.

3. Mark off 20 mile intervals and calculate the number of minutes it will take you to go 20 miles.

4. Circle the more important check points you intend to use.

You will never appreciate the importance of a properly marked map until the day you find yourself with an unmarked map, over strange terrain, with check points few and far between, with visibility limited and with your whereabouts in question. Get in the habit of always marking the line of flight, distance intervals, etc., on your map. It will save your neck some time when your gas is getting low and every minute counts.

# CROSS COUNTRY CHECKLIST

Following is a checklist of practical tips to have in mind during your cross country flights. These are "horse-sense" pointers collected from the experience of many, many flights. You'll avoid embarrassing mistakes if you'll go over them carefully.

### Leaving the Home Field

1. Be sure the airplane is ready. Set your altimeter correctly.

2. Have your map properly folded and in front of you at all times. Turn the map so that points on the map are lined up with points on the ground. It's easier to find check points that way.

3. Know how to read your compass. If doubtful, learn how before you leave the ground. Don't fly in the opposite direction as a few students have done.

4. Get set immediately after you have cleared the home airdrome. Climb to your assigned altitude in the vicinity of the field, level off, set controls, and trim the airplane for cruising flight. Get set on the right heading and stay on it.

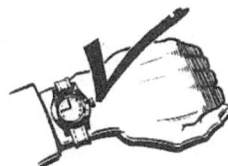

5. Be sure to note "Time Off." All time and distance calculations will be based on it. One approved method is to climb to cruising altitude over the field and then read your "Time Off."

6. Keep your radio turned up "Loud" and keep your headset on. Don't take it off and hang it on the primer or oil dilution handle or the compass will not read accurately.

### First Check Point

1. Don't expect your check point to pop up until you've been in the air long enough to reach it. Take a look at your watch—time and distance are buddies.

2. When you reach the check point, check your heading and if you are to one side of the point, change the heading. Remember that

the common fault is to over-correct and that you will seldom need to correct more than 10°. Estimate the change—don't try to do a lot of paper work in flight.

## An Easy Method

Remember the quick method of estimating error in your heading. When 60 miles out, one mile off course equals one degree off course. Thus, after 60 miles, if you are 5 miles off course to the right a correction of 5° to the left will head you parallel to your course. A correction of 10° to the left would bring you back to your course within another 60 miles. Then you should make another correction of 5° to the right to re-establish your on-course heading.

This works proportionately for different distances and the easy way to figure it is to always think in terms of 60 miles. Thus if you are 1 mile to the left of your course, 10 miles out, you would be 6 miles to the left when 60 miles out or 6° off course to the left. Knowing this, you can correct 6° right to parallel your course; or correct 12° right and fly 10 miles to get back to your course and then correct 6° left to re-establish the correct on-course heading.

3. Also compare your actual groundspeed with your estimated speed. For instance, if you arrive at the first check point 20 miles out 2 minutes late, you know that you'll probably be 10 minutes late in 100 miles, etc. At 120 miles per hour you are traveling 2 miles a minute so that 2 or 3 minutes variation from your estimated time of arrival at a point won't matter much. Correct your time-table mentally, as you go along, from point to point and make sure of each check point. When check points are close enough together, and distinctive enough, it is almost impossible to get lost.

## During the Flight

1. **Believe your compass** rather than your sense of direction and hold steadily to your heading. But use common sense about the compass. It can easily be off a few degrees one way or the other. Check your heading against check points and if you are **sure** the compass is off one way or the other, modify your heading accordingly.

2. Don't keep fooling with mixture control and throttle. What you want is a constant cruising rpm throughout the flight.

3. Keep your head out of the cockpit. Don't get lost in map reading and forget to watch your heading and the sky ahead. There are many airplanes in the air these days.

4. Keep your ears open for special radio instructions. There may be some reason to call you back.

5. Hold to your assigned altitude unless forced down by an overcast. Remember that Contact Flight Rules require you always to stay 500 ft. below clouds and 500 ft. above the ground except when landing, etc.

6. If ceiling gets below 1,000 ft. above the ground, turn around and come back or land at a nearby airdrome and report by telephone.

7. Keep track of the wind direction and velocity. You have to know these in case of a forced landing.

## Caution:

**DON'T LET YOUR MAPS BLOW OUT!**

**KEEP THE CANOPY CLOSED WHEN**

**HANDLING YOUR MAPS**

**AND ANCHOR YOUR MAPS WHEN**

**YOU OPEN THE CANOPY.**

**IN 60 MILES, 1 MILE OFF COURSE = 1° OFF COURSE**

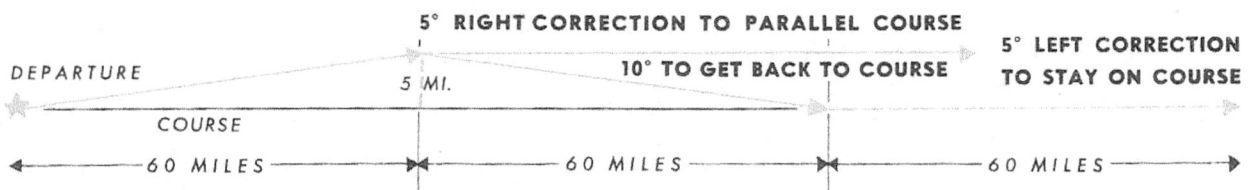

5° RIGHT CORRECTION TO PARALLEL COURSE

10° TO GET BACK TO COURSE

5° LEFT CORRECTION TO STAY ON COURSE

DEPARTURE

5 MI.

COURSE

◀—— 60 MILES ——▶◀—— 60 MILES ——▶◀—— 60 MILES ——▶

## Fuel Procedure

Remember that an airplane engine won't run without fuel. Watch your fuel supply and keep tanks within 10 gallons of each other to prevent wing heaviness. Use the standard procedure for warm-up and take-off. Then switch between right and left tanks. The reserve setting leaves you about 30 minutes of fuel. Save it for emergencies and when you go "On Reserve," immediately start looking for a place to land.

## So You're Lost!

You are not lost until you **think you are lost** and give up trying to find yourself. You've got a map, a time-table, a compass, and a radio. **Use them!**

Think it through. You started for a point. Unless you flew in the opposite direction, you are either short of the point, beyond it, or to one side or the other. Don't give up. The pilot who gets excited, confused, and gives up can get lost over his home field. Here are pointers on what to do when you miss your check point!

1. Use common sense. Stay on the right heading to be sure your check point isn't going to show up in a few moments. Don't start wandering around the sky aimlessly. Keep flying that airplane. Have you miscalculated time or deviated from your course? Consider all the angles.

2. Start working between your map and the landscape. If you can locate one distinct landmark on the ground and on the map, you'll know where you are.

3. If near a town, look for the name on buildings or water tanks. Look at the road pattern, for water nearby, etc.

4. If you can't find yourself, try to call the home airdrome, the control airplane or another airplane and explain your situation.

5. As a last resort shoot a railroad station.

6. If you are getting low on fuel or if there is danger that darkness will overtake you, pick the best available field, drag it, and land. Don't wait until you are out of fuel or until it is too dark to land. After landing, follow the same procedure as specified for a forced landing.

## Procedure at Destination

1. Check in with the control ship by radio to get landing instructions as soon as you are in the vicinity of your destination.

2. Before losing altitude, double check your mixture control in FULL RICH position.

3. Observe traffic carefully. It will usually be to the left around the field unless you are instructed otherwise.

4. Make one circle around the field at 1,500 ft. to determine wind direction, layout of runways, obstructions on and around the field, and to plan your approach.

5. Keep radio loud to hear all instructions from the ground.

6. If in doubt about obstructions or about the condition of the field, use a regular landing approach and drag the field into the wind.

7. In case of radio failure, there will be a pre-arranged signal to tell you whether or not to land.

8. All landings will be from a power-on approach. After landing, park as instructed, fill out Form 1, and await instructions! Remember that an airplane won't fly without fuel.

9. Take off when instructed, circle the field to the left unless otherwise directed, and climb immediately to your assigned altitude.

10. Follow the same procedure in the return flight as in the flight out. Keep alert. It's just as easy to lose your way going back as coming out.

### Forced Landing Procedure

Here are useful tips in case a Forced Landing is necessary.

Quickly check to see if you can't re-start the engine. If this fails and a suitable field is available, execute the forced landing in exactly the same way you have practiced Simulated Forced Landings.

Over rough or wooded terrain, where there is no suitable field, bail out if altitude permits. If you are too low to bail out or if a high wind makes bailing out inadvisable, take these precautions:

Maneuver to land into the wind but avoid low turns. Turn the selector valve off and pump the throttle a few times to get all the fuel out of the engine. Turn off all switches that might throw a spark . . . including the radio. Take off your goggles, be sure your safety belt is securely fastened, take off your radio headset and your cap if it has insignia on it. Open the canopy, lock the shoulder harness if available, and lower your seat to provide extra head room and to avoid head injuries. Do everything possible to slow down the airplane. Use full flaps, land directly into the wind, drop the airplane in slightly, and try to distribute the impact of landing.

### AFTER THE LANDING DO THE FOLLOWING:

1. Notify the home station immediately by radio, telephone or telegraph (Government Collect).

2. Direct telephone calls to your Group Commander, telegrams to the Commanding Officer_____Field.

Give this information:
Place. Tell exact location and type of field.
Cause of the landing.
Condition of personnel.
Condition of airplane.
How the pilot can be reached by telephone or telegraph.

3. Stay with the airplane until you receive instructions or assistance.

4. If injured, enlist help to send your message and to guard the airplane.

5. Don't take off until authorized by competent authority.

6. Don't land at the scene of a forced landing or a crash. Report it to the home airdrome or to an instructor.

# NIGHT NAVIGATION FLIGHTS

There is nothing at all difficult about night navigation if you learn all you can before leaving the ground and use your head. Carefully study the exact route to be followed, listen intently to what your instructor has to say, learn the radio procedure and how to check in over control points. For your convenience, here is a checklist of practical tips on night navigation.

### Preparation

1. Mark your maps clearly. Remember that you have to read them quickly in dim light. Figure headings exactly. Night flying is exact compass flying. Study the map carefully and try to visualize how the route will look at night.

2. Prepare a time-table that will tell you what headings to fly and how long to fly them. Write down only the headings and number of minutes for each leg. Brief yourself mentally on the time to look for prominent intermediate check points. Don't expect to do a lot of map reading in the air at night.

3. Have your map conveniently folded so it is easy to handle and fasten your time table securely to it so you will have only one item (the map) to hold.

4. Get a flashlight with a string on it so you can hang it around your neck, pencil type preferable. Red cellophane or paper fastened over the lense provides the best light for map reading.

### Leaving the Home Field

1. Remember all you learned about night flying. Adapt your eyes for night vision. Check to be sure all your lights and your radio are working. Keep your cockpit lights turned down low.

2. Climb to cruising altitude in the vicinity of the home field but be careful to avoid other ships that may be engaged in night

flying. Close your canopy when you are at cruising altitude above the field.

3. Establish the correct heading and note your time away from the field. Remember that night flying is compass, time, and distance flying. If you fly the right headings the right length of time, you can't go far wrong.

## During the Cross-Country

1. Don't start looking for check points before it is time for them to show up. You'll just confuse yourself. Fly that airplane straight and level, using your compass and instruments as necessary.

2. Keep your head out of the cockpit, keep your eyes shifting. There are other pilots on this same flight and you don't want to try to occupy their air space while they are still in it.

3. Each time, after you look at your map and before you look out of the cockpit, check your instruments to be sure you are straight and level.

4. Remember that your best friends on a night cross-country are your time-table, your compass, and your watch. Fly your heading for the specified length of time plus five minutes. Then, if you haven't reached the control point where you are to change your heading, change it anyhow, fly the next heading for the specified time and so on. If you merely fly the correct headings for the proper length of time, this will usually bring you back within sight of the home field.

## Use of Check Points

1. Roads are very easy to locate at night by watching for automobile headlights. Rivers and bodies of water are easy to see in the early evening and on nights when there is a moon. In preparing for a night mission, it is always well to mark plainly on the map any bodies of water that may be of help.

2. In checking towns from the air at night, practice judging the size of the town. It isn't easy to do, but frequently there will be a small town near a larger one which will give you an opportunity for comparison. A town will look larger earlier in the evening. Later the lights begin to go out and the town looks smaller from the air.

3. Mountains are clearly silhouetted against the evening sky and their dim outlines can usually be seen later at night. The relationship of a town or body of water to a mountain will give you a better check on your position than any single feature.

## Light Lines

Light lines are easily distinguished: they are the best check points of all because they tell you exactly where you are. A light line is a series of white rotating beacons 10 to 15 miles apart along an airway. Most beacons have a smaller red light which flashes its own identifying code letter six times a minute. The code letter is marked on your map

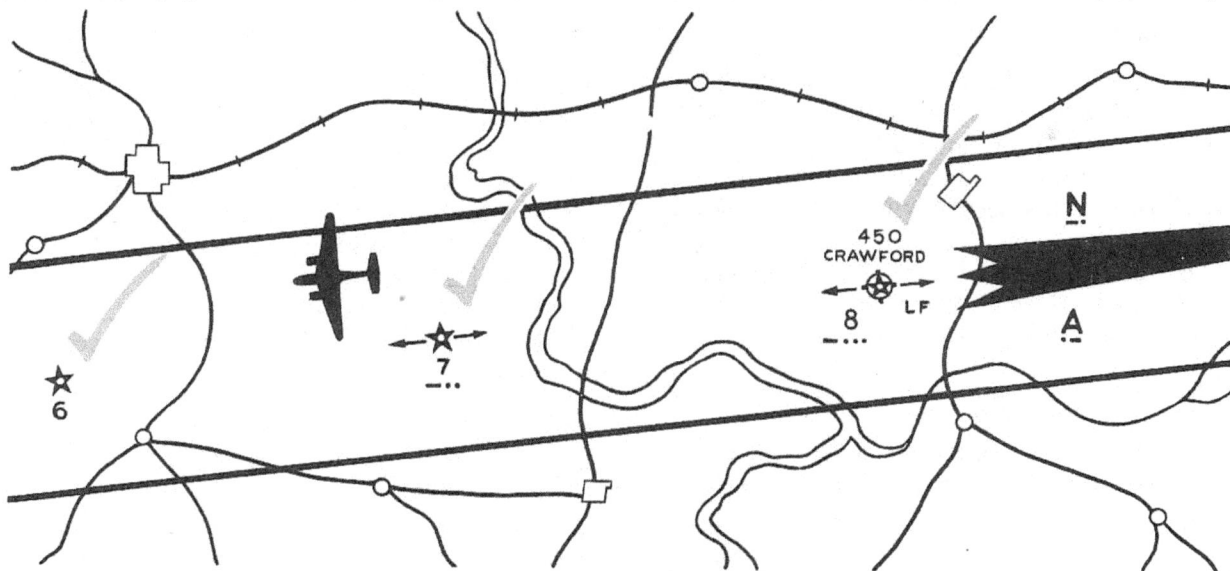

so that a single beacon will tell you your exact location along a given light line or the point at which you are crossing that light line.

Your map will also show you the magnetic heading of the beam which approximately parallels the light line. If necessary, you can distinguish a light line by flying along it long enough to determine its heading and by comparing that with the headings given on the map.

The identification signals of light line beacons are easiest to read when flying along parallel to the line of beacons at not too high an altitude. When you are flying at an angle to the light line, the signal becomes less easy to read. The majority of beacons flash a red identification signal, but some are only rotating beacons. Those marking CAA Intermediate fields flash their identification in green indicating landing facilities.

## Airport Beacons

Differences in airport beacons will sometimes tell you whether an airport is a commercial or Army field. Beacons at all commercial fields and at some Army fields are rotating white lights that look like searchlights. Most commercial fields have a flashing green light in addition to a rotating white light. Some of the older established Army fields have a white light beacon that blinks in all directions at the same time. When you see a blinking beacon of this type you know it marks an Army field.

## Weather

Stay below the overcast and don't fly into weather. It's dark enough at night without flying through clouds. Don't be startled if the air ahead is suddenly lighted up with a red glare. This occurs when your red passing light is reflected on clouds or mist. Glide below the clouds or reverse your course away from them. If you don't like the weather, turn around and come back to the home field or go to the closest airport and land.

## Emergency Procedure

If you become completely lost, keep flying your specified headings and watch for some distinguishing check point. If you spot a light line, fly along it until you identify the air-way and the beacon nearest you. Then fly along the line until you are at right angles to the home field and change course 90° to a heading that will take you home over the shortest distance. Or there may be a well-traveled highway that you can follow from the light line to your destination.

Don't get panicky under any circumstances. Don't bury your nose in your map. Don't keep changing headings so often that you completely lose track of the time (and therefore the distance) that you must have traveled along a given heading.

If lost, use your radio, state your predicament, tell where you think you are, what heading you are flying and what you intend to do. Although you may not be receiving, your message may be heard and a patrol ship can be sent after you.

If you have to land at a strange field, but can't establish radio contact, circle the field several times, flashing your landing lights. You should be able to tune in the tower though it may not hear your transmission since you will be sending on a training frequency. Watch out for traffic, wait until you get the green light or radio permission to land, and take your time on the landing. Make sure you know the wind and are landing in the right direction. Green lights always mark the approach end of the landing lane whether it is a field or a lighted runway. Red lights mark the other end of the runway. Always approach over the green lights.

If you are caught above the overcast and running out of gas in unknown country, don't try a let-down. And don't try to make a forced landing at night, except under such favorable circumstances that your chances for success are as good as in the daytime. When you go on the reserve tank, start getting out of the airplane. Have 3,000 or 4,000 ft. of altitude, point the airplane away from populated areas, set the trim tabs to hold it straight and level, and bail out. Don't wait until the engine quits and you lose control of the airplane.

## Instrument Flying

SEE THE LATEST EDITION OF T.O. 30-100A-1 (BASIC INSTRUMENT FLYING)

T.O.s 30-100B, C, D-1 deal with other phases of instrument flying and are good information sources.

# Parachutes

**All persons aboard Army Airplanes
will be equipped with standard-type parachutes
and will be instructed in their use**

### Before the Flight

Inspect your parachute. Remember, you may have to jump with it. Check the date of the last inspection. The packing interval should not exceed 60 days in the United States. Open the flap; make sure that the ripcord pins are not bent and that the seal is not broken. A bent pin or jammed wire may make it impossible to pull the ripcord. See that the corners of the pack are neatly stowed so that none of the silk is visible. See that the six or eight opening elastics are tight. Inspect each parachute you draw.

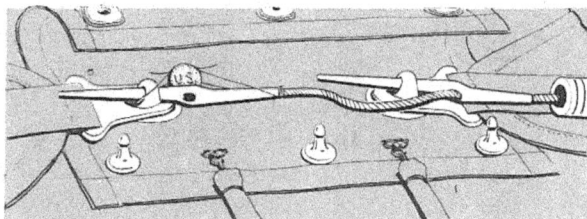

Put your parachute on and be sure the harness fits properly. The shoulder and chest straps should be snug without play; the chest buckle should be twelve inches below the chin. The leg straps should be snug. In fact, the harness should be comfortably snug when you are seated and disagreeably tight when you stand up.

### In Flight

If you find yourself in serious trouble:

**1.** Note your altimeter reading.

**2.** Estimate the altitude of the terrain below.

**3.** Decide on a minimum altitude or altimeter reading at which you (or you and your passenger) can safely bail out, taking into consideration the flight characteristics of the plane and the kind of trouble you are having.

CORRECT LANDING POSITION

**4.** If you are still in trouble when you reach that minimum altitude—bail out.

If you have a passenger, give him as much warning as possible. Let him know that it may be necessary to bail out.

### Bailing Out of Single-Engine Trainer

**1.** Open the cockpit canopy, or, if necessary, the emergency exit.

**2.** Slow the airplane as much as possible.

**3.** Disconnect your radio headset, etc.

**4.** Release your safety belt and shoulder harness.

**5.** Dive out and down. Often you can go out flat, onto the wing, and slide head first off the trailing edge.

### Bailing Out in a Spin

A review of the opinions of experts and of successful bailouts indicates that the best way to bail out of the BT-13A spinning nose-down is to the inside of the spin. If unusual aerodynamic conditions make it difficult to get out of the airplane on the inside of the spin, go to the outside—but be especially careful to dive down to let the tail pass above you.

## CLEARING THE AIRPLANE

Probably the most important single act, in any parachute jump, is opening the parachute only **after** you are clear of the plane. **Wait** until you are well away from the airplane before you pull the ripcord. Keep your eyes open. Look around.

## PULLING THE RIPCORD

It is not complicated or difficult to get your parachute safely open. Just:

**1.** Straighten your legs and put your feet together to reduce the opening shock and to avoid tangling your harness.

**2.** Use both hands to grasp the ripcord housing.

**3.** Grab the ripcord handle with the right hand, and yank! Keep your eyes open and look at the ripcord as you pull it.

## THE DESCENT

About two seconds after you have pulled the ripcord, you will feel a sharp, strong tug as the canopy opens and bites the air.

Look up to see that the chute is fully open. If a suspension line traverses the top, or if the lines are twisted, manipulate the lines to remedy the fault.

Do not worry about oscillations. They will almost certainly occur on your way down, but are of minor consequence. Do not attempt to check them or to slip the parachute, as such maneuvers are useful only to experts, and are dangerous below 200 feet.

Make a quick estimate of your altitude by looking first at the ground below and then at the horizon. You will descend approximately 1,000 to 1,500 feet per minute.

Observe your drift by craning your neck forward and sighting the ground between your feet, keeping your feet parallel and using them as a driftmeter.

Face in the direction of your drift.

While you cannot steer your chute, you can turn your body in any desired direction. The body turn is the most useful maneuver you can learn because with it you can make certain that you land facing in the direction of your drift. It is simple and easy.

Study the pictures. Practice the body turn in a suspended harness if you get the chance. This description may sound backward to you. Note with special care how these turns are executed and simply say to yourself:

"To turn right, right hand behind my head."

"To turn left, left hand behind my head."

# HOW TO MAKE BODY TURNS

**TO TURN YOUR BODY TO THE RIGHT:**

1 Reach up behind your head with your right hand and grasp the left risers.

2 Reach across in front of your head with your left hand and grasp the other risers. Your hands are now crossed, the right hand behind, and in each you have two risers.

3 Pull simultaneously with both hands; this will cross the risers above your head and turn your body to the right below them. You can readily turn 45, 90, or 180 degrees by varying the pull.

**Remember, to turn right, put your right hand behind and grab the opposite risers. To turn to the left, reverse this procedure.**

In the descent, start your body turn high enough to allow you to master it. Once you have made the turn, you will find that you can control your direction of drift perfectly. Hold the turn, or slowly ease up if necessary, to bring you in facing downwind. Continue to hold the risers, twisted or not as the case may be, and ride right on into the ground.

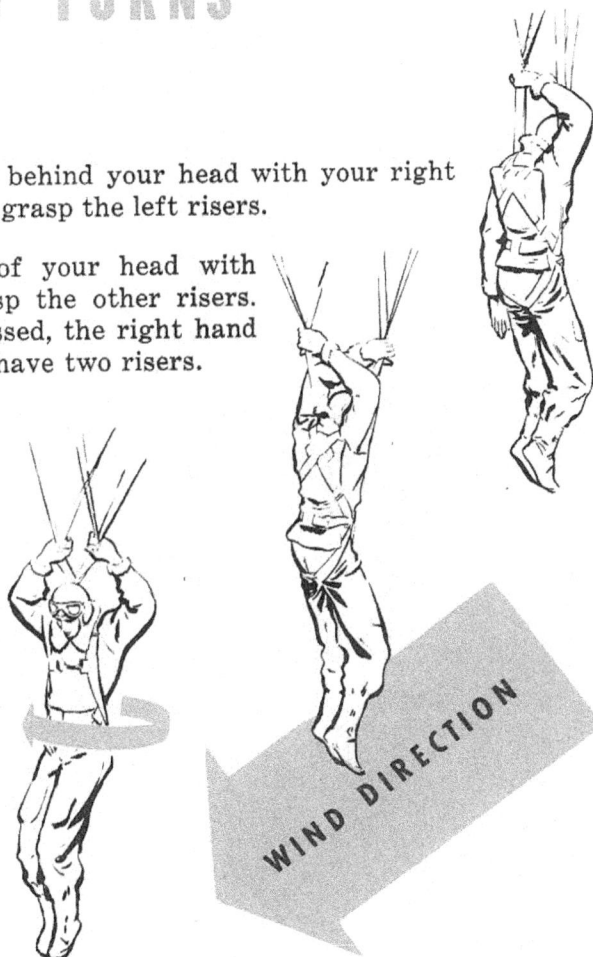

WIND DIRECTION

# THE LANDING

## Normal Landing

Whether you have made a body turn or not, keep your hands above your head, grasping the risers.

Look at the ground at a 45-degree angle, not straight down.

Set yourself for the landing by placing your feet together and slightly bending your knees, so that you will land on the balls of your feet. Don't be limp; don't be rigid.

Relax, and keep your feet firmly together with your knees slightly bent, and your hands grasping the risers above. Now hold everything and ride on into the ground, drifting face forward.

At the moment of impact, fall forward or sideways in a tumbling roll to reduce shock.

## Abnormal Landings

If there is a strong wind blowing across the ground when you land, do two things.

First, make certain that you carry out the procedures described above for a normal landing, including the body turn to face you exactly in your direction of drift.

High Wind

Second, once you are down, roll over on your stomach and haul in hand over hand on the suspension lines nearest the ground. Keep right on pulling them in until you grab silk. Then drag in the skirt of the canopy to spill the air and collapse the chute. If you can't manage this maneuver on your face, go over onto your back. Haul in the suspension lines until you can grasp the bottom edge of the canopy, then spill the chute.

Trees

Tree landings are usually the easiest of all. If you see that you are going to come into a tree, drop the risers, cross your arms in front of your head, and bury your face in the crook of an elbow. You can see under your folded forearm. Keep your feet and knees together. If you get hung up high in a tree, consider first the possibility of immediate rescue before you try to climb down. Failing that, get out of the harness and cut the lines and risers to make a rope for climbing down.

If you see that you are going to come down in water, start getting ready at least 500 feet up.

1. Throw away anything you won't need.

2. Pull yourself back into the sling as far as possible.

3. Undo your chest strap by hooking a thumb beneath one of the vertical lift webs, pushing firmly across your chest to loosen the cross webbing so that you can undo the snap.

4. Free the leg straps by doubling up first one leg and then the other, unsnapping the fasteners each time. Hang on to the risers.

5. When your feet touch the water, throw your arms straight up and shrug your shoulders out of the harness, so that the canopy will blow clear.

6. Inflate the Mae West.

Use a knife to cut yourself free of harness, and suspension lines, if necessary.

### High Tension Wires

High tension wires are frequently high above the ground and strung about six feet apart. If you find yourself coming into such wires, extend your hands above your head, with the palms flat against the inside of the risers to avoid contact. Keep your feet and knees together. Turn your head into one shoulder to protect your face. Streamline your body as much as possible so that you will fall straight through. The chute may collapse, but will open again enough to break the fall. Even if you get hung up, remember that silk is a non-conductor and wait for rescue.

### Night Jumps

As soon as your chute is open, prepare for a normal landing. Since you cannot see the ground on a dark night, you want to be ready to make contact at any moment. Get your feet and knees together, your legs slightly bent. Hang onto the risers above your head and wait for contact.

## TAKE CARE OF YOUR PARACHUTE

The longer you fly the more you will "pamper" a parachute. Inspect the pack whenever you go up. If dirt, grease, or water has marked it, return the chute to supply. Look for breaks or signs of abuse.

Don't dump it on the floor. Never kneel on it, or carry it jammed against your hip. Don't leave it in the airplane where moisture may reach the pack. Take care of your parachute. It's life insurance. Don't let that policy lapse.

# Index

FOR PURPOSES OF TRAINING, CERTAIN VARIANCES FROM AAF TECHNICAL
ORDERS HAVE BEEN INDICATED IN THIS MANUAL PENDING DECISIONS ON
PROCEDURE FROM HIGHER HEADQUARTERS

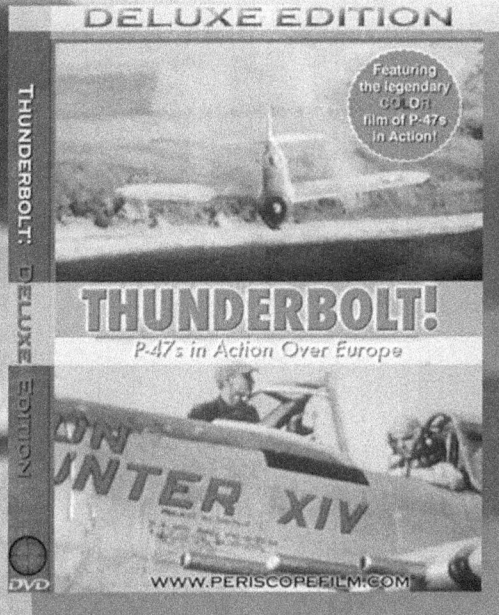

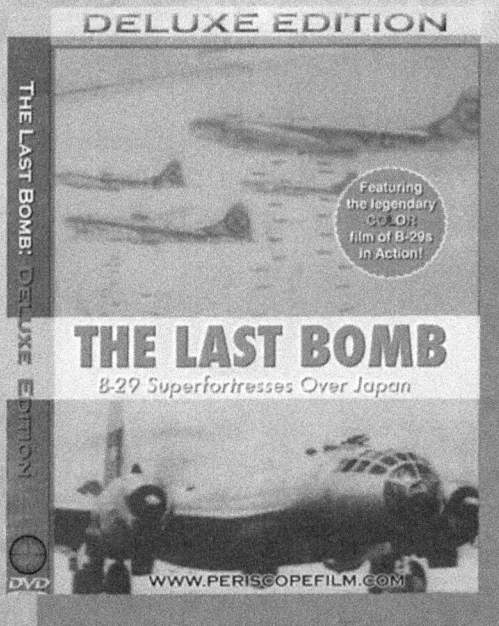

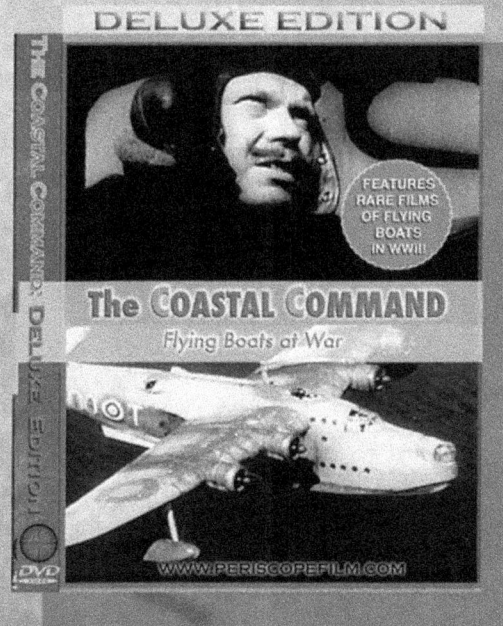

# EPIC BATTLES
# OF WWII

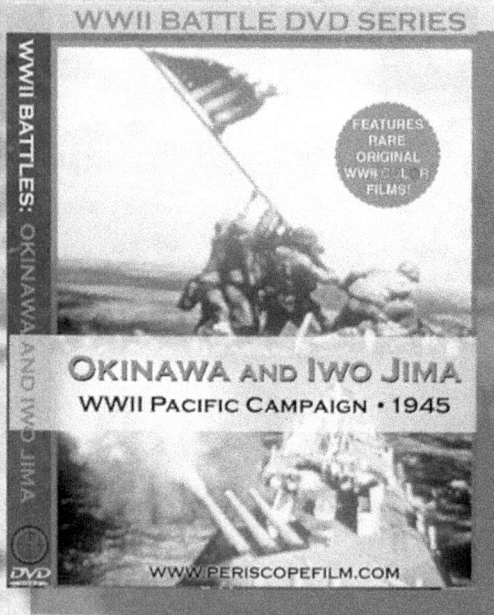

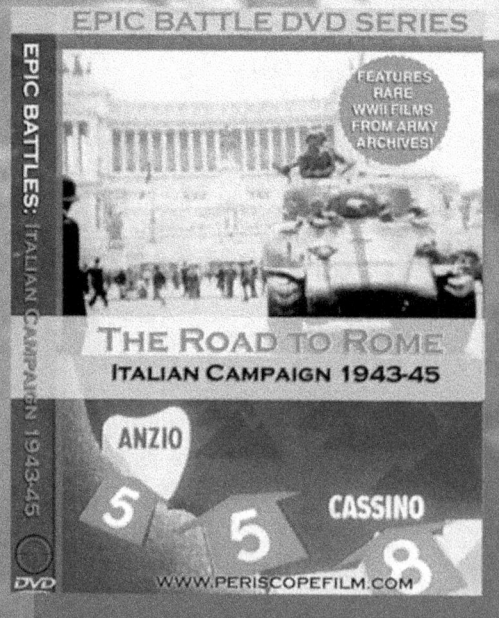

# NOW AVAILABLE ON DVD!